Battling Boredom Part 2

Drive boredom out of your classroom—and keep it out—with the student engagement strategies in this book. In the first *Battling Boredom*, bestselling author Bryan Harris offered strategies on beginning a lesson, ending a lesson, small group work, and large group work. Now in *Battling Boredom Part 2*, Harris teams up with technology integration expert and former teacher Lisa Bradshaw to provide additional strategies on new topics such as academic talk, feedback, writing, classroom technology, and more. You'll learn how to:

- Increase the quality and effectiveness of feedback to boost student performance.
- Engage students in meaningful reflection with writing prompts and exercises.
- Re-energize a lethargic class using movement-based activities.
- Integrate technology to create a more enriching classroom experience for students.
- Encourage students to speak up, share their ideas, and talk about their learning.

With this toolbox of instructional strategies, you'll have even more ways to end student boredom before it begins, resulting in class time that's more efficient, more educational, and loads more fun!

Bryan Harris is the Director of Professional Development and Public Relations for the Casa Grande Elementary School District in Arizona.

Lisa Bradshaw is the Director of Information Technology for the Casa Grande Elementary School District in Arizona.

Other Eye On Education Books Available from Routledge (www.routledge.com/eyeoneducation)

Battling Boredom [Part 1]
99 Strategies to Spark Student Engagement
Bryan Harris

75 Quick and Easy Solutions to Common Classroom Disruptions
Bryan Harris and Cassandra Goldberg

Creating a Classroom Culture That Supports the Common Core
Teaching Questioning, Conversation Techniques, and Other Essential Skills
Bryan Harris

Motivating Struggling Learners
10 Ways to Build Student Success
Barbara R. Blackburn

Rigor Is Not a Four-Letter Word, 2nd Edition
Barbara R. Blackburn

Rigor and Assessment in the Classroom
Barbara R. Blackburn

Classroom Instruction from A to Z, 2nd Edition
Barbara R. Blackburn

The Flexible ELA Classroom
Practical Tools for Differentiated Instruction in Grades 4–8
Amber Chandler

Passionate Learners, 2nd Edition
How to Engage and Empower Your Students
Pernille Ripp

Passionate Readers
The Art of Reaching and Engaging Every Child
Pernille Ripp

Battling Boredom Part 2

Even More Strategies to Spark Student Engagement

Bryan Harris and Lisa Bradshaw

Routledge
Taylor & Francis Group

NEW YORK AND LONDON

First published 2018
by Routledge
711 Third Avenue, New York, NY 10017

and by Routledge
2 Park Square, Milton Park, Abingdon, Oxon, OX14 4RN

Routledge is an imprint of the Taylor & Francis Group, an informa business

Library of Congress Cataloging-in-Publication Data
A catalog record has been requested

ISBN: 978-1-138-71476-2 (hbk)
ISBN: 978-0-415-40316-0 (pbk)
ISBN: 978-1-315-22889-1 (ebk)

Typeset in Palatino
by Deanta Global Publishing Services, Chennai, India

Contents

Acknowledgments

Bryan

Every written work is a collaborative effort, regardless of how many authors are officially listed. *Battling Boredom Part 2* is no exception and I am tremendously grateful to the talented, thoughtful, and gracious people who have supported this project and my career in general.

- To my wife, Becky, and my sons, Andrew and Jeremy, for being a constant source of support and encouragement. Life gives us challenges now and then, but I am blessed to be taking the journey with them.

- To the teachers, administrators, and paraprofessionals across the country who have invited me to their schools and districts, a giant *thank you*. Sharing these ideas is a privilege and I appreciate the hard-working educators who daily tackle the challenges of battling boredom.

- To Lisa Bradshaw, my collaborator and partner on this project, another giant *thank you*. This book is better because of your patience, advice, ideas, and feedback.

- To Lauren Davis, ever-patient editor and encourager, thanks for prompting me to start this project and for guiding me through another book.

Lisa

Without the privilege of working with so many wonderful, talented educators, I would not have grown into the educator I am. I thank them for the hours spent meeting with me, listening to me, reflecting with me, and allowing me to try new ideas in their classrooms (many of those ideas are presented in this book).

I would be remiss, however, to not express my deepest gratitude to those who have offered me the most support in the journey throughout my career thus far:

- My husband, Lee, for the many years of listening, talking, advice, encouragement, and love. He supports me in anything I set out to accomplish. I could not have accomplished it all without the support you've given me. My "B Boys," Brody and Brom, who are my guinea pigs at home trying out the new apps, websites, and gadgets I find and are the inspiration to make education fun. The three of you are my happy.

- My parents, Roberta and Dwight, who always support me and push me to do my best—and taught me that I can accomplish anything with hard work.

- The administration and staff in the Casa Grande Elementary School District have given me incredible opportunities to grow in my career and have pushed me to think, question, and look for what is best for our students each day—Dr Frank Davidson, Dr Barbara Wright, Dr Bryan Harris, Andrea Munoz, Leslie Kramer, and all the other talented and supportive staff I've had the great privilege working with over the years.

About the Authors

■ Bryan Harris, EdD

Bryan Harris serves as the Director of Professional Development and Public Relations for the Casa Grande Elementary School District in Arizona. He holds a Bachelor of Science degree in Education and a Master of Educational Leadership degree from Northern Arizona University. In 2013, he earned a doctorate (EdD) from Bethel University in Minnesota after studying factors impacting new teacher retention. He also holds a certification in brain-based learning from Jensen Learning Corporation.

Having served in many roles in education—from a classroom teacher to a principal, and now a central office leader—Bryan understands the challenges teachers and school leaders face as they strive to meet the needs of all students. Each year, he speaks to thousands of educators all over the country on the topics of student engagement, motivation, classroom management, and brain-based learning. He is author or coauthor of several books, including the popular 2010 book *Battling Boredom*. He can be reached at www.bryan-harris.com.

■ Lisa Bradshaw

Lisa Bradshaw serves as the Director of Information Technology for the Casa Grande Elementary School District in Casa Grande, Arizona. She works with K-12 teachers, providing staff development, to improve student engagement and achievement through the use of technology in the classroom. She encourages teachers to integrate technology in authentic manners by promoting high interest, project-based learning and digital literacy.

Lisa has worked in education since 2001, spending 9 years in the classroom as an elementary and middle school teacher prior to moving into professional development, with Dr Bryan Harris, as the Technology Integration Specialist in her district for 6 years. Lisa completed her Bachelor's degree in Elementary Education in 2000 from the University of Arizona and completed her Master's degree in Educational Technology in 2006 from Northern Arizona University. She can be reached at www.techin10.com.

Introduction to
Battling Boredom Part 2

In Harper Lee's classic novel *To Kill A Mockingbird*, the main character and narrator of the story is a young girl named Scout who is equal parts curious about the world and insightfully honest about what she observes. In one of the more memorable scenes of the book, she describes an interaction with her cousin Francis to which most of us can relate. She calls him "the most boring child I ever met," and declared that "Talking to Francis gave me the sensation of settling slowly to the bottom of the ocean." Haven't we all been in situations where we were *so* bored we felt as if we were "settling slowly to the bottom of the ocean"? While Scout was not describing a formal learning or classroom environment, her feelings resonate with a lot of our students.

Let's be honest, some of our students (perhaps even *many* of our students) get bored easily and often in our classrooms. National studies show that alarmingly high numbers of students report being bored in school and that this has a massive impact on learning (Vogel-Walcutt et al., 2012). And battling boredom can be an immense challenge for educators who feel increasingly pressured to teach more and more material in less and less time. Some schools and classrooms have found themselves in a vicious cycle—teachers need to cover more and more material with students who seem less and less engaged. Fortunately, we know what works to engage students and this book is full of strategies, methods, and techniques that will make learning engaging, meaningful, and memorable.

When *Battling Boredom* was first published in 2010, Bryan shared the story of a third grade student, named Chad, who exclaimed "School is boring!" This started him on a 10-plus-year journey to discover what truly engages students in deep, meaningful learning. Since then, the research on student boredom and engagement has continued to flourish. A wide range of academic disciplines—from neuroscientists to educators to economists—have studied issues related to boredom and engagement and have offered some fascinating insights. Consider some of what we know about boredom and engagement:

- The 2009 High School Survey of Student Engagement reported that over 60 percent of high school students said they were bored in class on a daily basis. When asked why they were bored, over 80 percent of them said it was because the material was not interesting.

- The number of students who report being engaged in school drops dramatically as they get older. In a 2012 Gallup poll, 76 percent of elementary students reported being engaged in school. That number drops to 61 percent in middle school and a shocking 44 percent in high school. And it doesn't get any better in college. A 2009 study reported that 40 percent of first year college students said they were bored in class (Daniels, 2009).

- Students are 30 times more likely to be engaged in school when they report *agree* or *strongly agree* to the statements "My school is committed to building the strengths of each student" and "I have at least one teacher who makes me excited about the future" (Gallup, 2013).

- In a unique 2014 study, University of Virginia researcher, Timothy Wilson, found that 67 percent of college males and 25 percent of college females voluntarily gave themselves a mild electric shock rather than experience mental boredom.

- Boredom is a stressful mental state that results in decreased activity in the brain's pre-frontal cortex and more activity in the amygdala. When someone is bored, it is not unusual for them to respond emotionally rather than rationally (Parasuraman & Jiang, 2012). Judy Willis, a neurologist turned educator, says that when the brain becomes bored, the pre-frontal cortex "loses" communication with the rest of the brain resulting in involuntary fight, flight, or freeze responses in the amygdala, which controls emotional responses.

- During a boring task, the brain's Default Mode Network (DMN) often kicks in. The DMN is associated with autobiographical memories and actions such as reminiscing and daydreaming.

- When someone is bored, there are lower levels of dopamine in their brain. Dopamine is a neurotransmitter associated with attention, motivation, and reward-based activity. Sometimes referred to as the "feel good" neurotransmitter, it also plays a key role in learning (Zeld et al., 2008).

- We might really be boring our kids to a slow death. A 2010 study found that people who complained of boredom were more likely to die young. In addition, bored individuals had higher levels of heart disease (Britton & Shipley, 2010).

While some academic background is insightful and informative, our experience tells us that most teachers battle boredom in one form or another on a daily basis. We know it because we see it every day and what motivates us the most is finding and sharing effective instructional strategies that make a difference for teachers and students.

■ What Is Boredom and Engagement?

Battling Boredom (2010) offered educators some concrete definitions and tons of specific strategies for classroom use. However, definitions of boredom and engagement can vary widely in the academic research so a quick review of definitions and meanings is worth considering.

As stated previously, boredom is an emotional state. When we are bored, we feel it. The French have a term for it; they call it *ennui*. It is that overwhelming feeling of listlessness bordering on hopelessness. All of us can relate to the feeling of being trapped in a situation that is irrelevant, meaningless, and uninteresting. Unfortunately, for many students that describes their school experience. They are trapped in situations that they perceive as meaningless. Personal perception is a key idea when attempting to understand boredom and engagement. While the content being presented by the teacher might very well be relevant to a student's future success, what matters most is that the student recognizes that fact. Relevance and meaning, like beauty, are in the eyes of the beholder.

In one of the best serious academic treatments of the concept of boredom, *The Definition, Assessment, and Mitigation of State Boredom within Educational Settings*, Jennifer Vogel-Walcutt and her colleagues (2012) stress that boredom results when an individual's skill level exceeds the challenge of the task in front of them or when there is little or no choice in how to complete those tasks. Their findings mesh well with a concept known as the *Control Value Theory of Emotions*, which states that boredom is likely to result when individuals are in a situation where they have little control and are faced with content that has little personal value. In classrooms, we often see students who are asked to learn things or complete tasks that have little meaning or value to them. In addition, students are often given very little choice or control over how to complete those tasks. In fact, Daniels and Tze (2014) call this the "perfect storm of boredom." It's practically a recipe; if you want to produce boredom within your students, give them no choice in how to complete a personally irrelevant task.

So, how do we define boredom and engagement? Classrooms are complicated places with lots of moving parts and more variables than can easily be measured so concrete definitions are sometimes a challenge. In *Battling Boredom* (2010), Bryan offered the following definition of boredom in the classroom: "A temporary emotional condition marked by disinterest in the information, context, or events provided by the teacher that may sometimes result in inappropriate behaviors." While that definition still seems accurate in light of more current research, we would make one small but significant update. The more we dig into the academic research and talk with teachers on the front lines, we realize that boredom is way more common than we want to admit and boredom is closely related to behavior. When students are in situations that they perceive as irrelevant, it often results in them making poor choices or engaging in inappropriate behaviors. As a result, we would change the word "sometimes" to "often." Bored students often do things that are inappropriate and result in behavior issues. Boredom not only impacts a student's ability to learn and remember, but bored students might very well become discipline problems.

Of course, merely understanding the nature of boredom is not our sole aim. We also want to understand the nature and characteristics of student engagement. In *Battling Boredom* (2010), Bryan defined engagement as "A state of emotional and cognitive willingness to participate in the task or learning goal." A key idea here is that, as educators, our goal is to get our students to commit to what we are asking them to do. This emotional and cognitive commitment is generated by things like relevance, meaning, novelty, choice, authentic tasks, positive relationships, social interaction, physical movement, and fun activities.

A lot has been written about the importance of student engagement and how to elicit it, but we particularly appreciate the perspective of the Gallup Organization as reflected in their 2015 report *Engaged Today—Ready for Tomorrow*. About student engagement they said, "Engaged students are excited about what's happening at their school and what they're learning. These students contribute to the learning environment, and they're psychologically committed to their school." That sounds like the dream scenario for teachers: excited students who contribute and commit to their learning. That same report highlighted how engaging learning environments foster hope in students. Hopeful students are positive about the future and can overcome obstacles and challenges as they strive to meet their learning goals.

As educators work to engage their students in meaningful learning, they need a deep and varied toolbox of instructional strategies. That is what we offer here: specific strategies with step-by-step directions for how to make learning come alive for students. However, before digging into those strategies, it is important to pause and consider the differences between authentic engagement and mere "on-task" behavior. Getting students to be on-task is not the goal; the goal is for them to be engaged in something meaningful that leads to learning. Don't get us wrong—on-task behavior is not a bad thing—but consider the fact that it is possible to be technically "on-task" but not actually engaged in learning. Mindlessly copying notes from a presentation is an example. So is sitting and listening to a long lecture. In those cases, students may appear to be on-task, but their minds are likely engaged in something entirely different than what the teacher had intended. As an analogy, consider that you can technically be on-task while driving a car but not mentally engaged in it. The big idea here is that we should not confuse on-task behavior with engaged learning.

■ Overview of *Battling Boredom Part 2*

The 2010 version of *Battling Boredom* offered engagement strategies and techniques for such topics as beginning a lesson, ending a lesson, whole group work, small group work, partner work, and movement, and even offered solutions for engaging reluctant learners. The strategies we offer in *Battling Boredom Part 2* supplement and build on that original work. However, *Battling Boredom Part 2* is not a revision of the 2010 book. Rather, here we offer strategies for new topics and categories not addressed in the first book. We have designed it to be a companion book that, like its older sibling, outlines specific strategies that are likely to increase the engagement level of students. In addition, the strategies we outline and describe will be relevant and applicable in a wide variety of grade levels and content areas. We have used these methods and techniques from primary grades through higher education with great success. Students of all ages respond to these strategies because they increase the likelihood of authentic engagement in the learning. Therefore, we offer step-by-step directions for strategies on the following topics:

- *Academic Talk*—This section will provide strategies and methods for getting students to talk about their learning. We know that when students talk, elaborate, explain, and share their ideas that they are more likely to be engaged and remember what they are learning.

- *Energizers*—Physically sedentary environments are not good for learning. The brain is designed to move and when students are given opportunities for structured movement, they engage more and remember more.

- *Feedback*—When students receive and use specific feedback they engage more in their learning, take more risks, and achieve at higher levels. If you want your students to learn more, ramp up the levels of specific, actionable feedback that they receive.

- *Questioning*—Asking questions is as old as school itself and there is a ton of research that supports the connection between questioning and student achievement. However, not all questioning strategies are equally effective at engaging students.

- *Technology*—All too often students have to power down their devices and technology when they walk into a classroom. The fact is that students are more likely to be engaged when they are using technology while learning.

- *Vocabulary*—Fluency, competency, and achievement in a subject require a deep understanding of content-specific vocabulary. The strategies described in this section will engage students in learning, remembering, and understanding vocabulary.

- *Writing*—The process of writing is the process of thinking. One of the best ways to engage students in deep, meaningful thinking is to ask them to write about their learning. The strategies outlined in this section focus on writing to learn as opposed to learning to write.

- *Strategies that Don't Work*—In this section, we offer a unique look at some "classic" classroom strategies that actually impede or outright stop learning and engagement. These are strategies that should be removed from the "toolbox."

Another new feature of *Battling Boredom Part 2* is the inclusion of a brief introduction to each of the sections described above. Those introductions will provide some background, research, definitions, and considerations for the use of the strategies. If you are hungry for easy-to-use, relevant, and effective student engagement strategies, we invite you to dive in and expand your repertoire.

Part One

Academic Talk

Key Idea: *Academic talk and academically focused conversations are powerful and effective ways to boost student engagement. When students spend time talking about what they are learning, they become more engaged and they remember more of what they are learning. Quite simply, a quiet classroom where students spend the majority of their time sitting and listening will not lead to engagement, deep learning, or long-term memory.*

In the 2014 book, *Creating a Classroom Culture that Supports the Common Core*, Bryan wrote extensively about the power and impact of academic conversations as they relate to student engagement and achievement, particularly in light of the expectations of the Common Core Standards. While a review of that book is not necessary here, it is important to take a moment to provide some basic definitions and insights into the role of academic talk.

♦ Academic talk can be defined as student talk that builds and deepens content knowledge, enhances skill development, and engages students in the life of the classroom. The key idea here is that the talk—the conversations, the dialogue, the discussions— are being done *by the students*. Far too often, the primary voice in a classroom is that of the teacher. While listening certainly plays a role in learning, too many teachers assume that listening is *all* students have to do in order to remember something. We remember something when we interact with it in multiple ways; we must listen, read, write, watch, think, question, and talk about what we are learning. In fact, when students talk, particularly when they are given the chance to teach and tell others about what they are learning, they remember far more (Nestojko et al., 2014).

♦ The research supporting the role of talk and conversation, as it relates to student achievement, is well established (Zwiers & Crawford, 2011). Still, far too many classrooms are places that value silence above all. Unfortunately, too many teachers view student talk as either unnecessary or an impediment to learning. We cannot make it much clearer than this: if you want students to be engaged and to remember more of the content, get them to talk. A lot. Students should be given many opportunities, on a daily basis, to talk about their learning with peers, with the teacher, with other adults, and even to themselves! Harvey "Smokey" Daniels, outstanding teacher, author, and teller-like-it-is, states that students should be talking with a partner "at least 8 times per hour" (Daniels, 2013). A classroom that places a premium on passive, silent compliance may give the impression of engagement, but it's a house of cards. True engagement requires some aspect of talk and conversation.

♦ The ability to have an effective, focused, and successful academic conversation is a learned skill. Unfortunately, many students come to school without excellent examples nor extensive background experiences in the art of conversation. As a result, it is of critical importance that teachers provide clear models of successful academic talk. This cannot be understated—modeling is essential. Do not assume that all students know how to have a focused conversation, much less an academic one. Make sure that some sort of modeling is a part of every strategy you attempt to utilize.

♦ Academically focused conversations help to make learning self-evident. That is, when you have a conversation with someone, it becomes very clear, very quickly, how well you know something. If you have a depth of understanding about something, you are typically able to talk in more detail about it. If your knowledge is shallow, conversations tend to be very short. When a learner becomes self-aware, they become more engaged. When a student is able to honestly reflect and say to themselves, "As a result of that discussion, I realize that I really do not know this content very well," they are more likely to become engaged and motivated to learn the content.

♦ Listening to student conversations provides an outstanding source of informal assessment data. If you want to know how well, or how deeply, your students know something, listen to them talk about it. To paraphrase a semi-famous quote, "I thought they were smart until they started talking."

♦ Our belief is that student talk and student conversation should be a central feature of every classroom. But, we also realize the challenges teachers face. More than once we have heard teachers say something like, "Getting students to talk is not a problem. They love to talk. In fact, they talk too much. They talk about everything except what they are supposed to be talking about. Do you have any ideas for how to get them to stop talking?" For most teachers, this is part of their reality. The fact that kids like to talk is a good thing. The art of teaching is knowing your students and having a solid, thoughtful classroom management plan. As you work to focus student talk on academic subjects, consider these three questions:

1. *What is your own personal tolerance level?* Some teachers, by nature or personality, simply prefer a quiet environment. Other teachers don't mind the noise. The point is that you need to reflect and think about your own tolerances and learn to adjust them to best meet the needs of your students. The fact is that a constantly noisy, chaotic classroom is not good for students and neither is a constantly silent one. Effective teachers adjust their own preferences and tolerances for the benefit of their students.

2. *Do you plan and prepare for student talk?* When planning and designing lessons, student talk opportunities need to be included. Focused academic conversations rarely happen by chance. Student talk should not be an add-on or an alternative when all the other "real" learning activities are completed. Furthermore, student talk should not be a privileged activity for those "good" students who can handle the responsibility.

3. *Are you debriefing and giving feedback to students?* Students need guidance, feedback, and direction about their content knowledge in addition to their effectiveness at having conversations. When students are engaged in academic talk opportunities, teachers need to move around the room and provide direction, guidance, questions, praise, and feedback during the conversations. In fact, some of the busiest times a teacher will have in the classroom is when students are having their conversations.

We'd like to make one final point about the power of academic talk. Think about a topic you personally know well, something about which you have a deep knowledge and good long-term memory. For Bryan, that would be topics related to how the brain learns. For Lisa, that would be how technology impacts student engagement. There are a variety of factors that have led to our depth of knowledge in these areas. No doubt our interest and curiosity play a major role. The fact that we read a lot helps. We also both write extensively on those topics. Certainly, we have had excellent teachers and role models. But, we challenge you to consider the fact that we know these topics so well *primarily* because we talk about them, a lot. A day rarely goes by when Lisa is not talking about technology to someone. Bryan rarely goes a week without leading a professional development session or conducting a class where he gets to talk about the brain. Our depth of knowledge has been built on a foundation of talk. And it is the same for anything you know well. If you have a depth of knowledge in something, there is a likelihood that you talk a lot about it. Knowing that your own personal depth of knowledge has been built by talking, allow your students the same opportunities.

■ Overview

Concrete, physical objects and items from everyday life can serve as a powerful source of student dialogue and discussion.

■ Step by Step

1. Prior to the lesson, collect items and objects that are related to the objective, or that can be used to illustrate major concepts or ideas. For example, when studying the agricultural south prior to the Civil War, collect some raw, uncleaned cotton directly from a farm.

2. Remind students of the lesson or unit focus and major objectives.

3. Tell students that they'll get a chance to look at, touch, feel, and experience something that will help them to understand the topic being studied. In the example above, provide each student with a small amount of the raw cotton and ask them to handle it, attempt to clean it, and imagine what it would have been like to have to harvest and clean raw cotton. Experiences such as this help the learning to become more vivid and "real."

4. Distribute, show, or allow students to interact with the objects.

5. Lead students to discuss the different objects and how they relate to the learning objectives. If needed, prompt students with specific questions such as, "How would this item represent a concept we've discussed?"

■ Tips and Variations

♦ Unlike the example given in Step 1, it is not necessary to get enough of the same objects for every student. Instead, consider collecting several different examples of items and placing them into groups for students.

♦ Some teachers have chosen to create a "memory box" that includes several items that represent something about the concept or topic being studied. For example, when reading a work of historical fiction, the box might include examples of clothing from the time or items a fictional character might have used.

♦ Story boxes are a popular literary strategy for young learners. These boxes include physical items represented in the story students are reading. For example, when reading *Goodnight Moon* by Margaret Wise Brown, the following items are placed in a box and used before, during, or after the reading: phone, socks, balloon, bowl, and so on.

■ Overview

This strategy provides groups of three students with specific roles to play during a discussion.

■ Step by Step

1. Place students into groups of three and remind them of the lesson or unit objectives.

2. Assign each student with a letter—A, B, or C.

3. Tell students that they'll be taking about 5 minutes to have a small group discussion. Tell students that the discussion will require that each student play a specific role according to the letter they've been assigned. Student A will be the person who describes the concept, Student B will be the one who asks questions about the concept, and Student C will be the one who offers ideas and answers questions about the concept.

4. Display or provide a handout or cards to students that lists the responsibilities of each role along with some sentence stems.

   Student A describes or defines the term or concept:

   "We are discussing __________. It can be defined as …"

   "I know 3 things about ______. To start, I would say …"

   Student B asks questions about the term or concept:

   "What would happen if …"

   "If ______ was changed, what would be the result?

   Student C offers ideas or answers questions about the term or concept:

   "I would answer your question by saying …"

   "Here is another example of ______."

5. During students' discussions, move around the room monitoring and providing feedback to students.

6. Depending on the age and maturity level of your students, provide them with another topic or prompt them to conduct another round of discussions.

■ Tips and Variations

♦ Like most of the strategies found throughout this book, students will benefit from a model of this strategy prior to being asked to do it themselves. In this case, bring three students to the front of the class and have them model what the process looks like. Use that model to debrief with students about what to expect and what to do if they seem to get stuck.

♦ **Differentiation Connection**: Consider varying the sentence stems that students use during their role. Many teachers also provide students with three different terms or topics and ask students to switch roles during each "round" of discussions.

■ Overview

Much like Sentence Starters or Sentence Stems, this strategy utilizes specific words or phrases to encourage students to elaborate on their ideas, thoughts, and key learning. Many conversations, even interesting and engaging ones, experience a natural lull during the interaction that leaves most people to assume that the conversations are over. However, with carefully placed conversation extenders, students can learn to dig deeper in their conversations.

■ Step by Step

1. Prior to the lesson, teach students about the art of conversation and dialogue. Help them to understand that most conversations will experience lulls and periods of silence where it is easy to assume that the conversation is over. However, tell them most conversations can be extended and lengthened with specific questions and prompts.

2. Remind students of the objectives of the lesson or unit.

3. Provide a prompt, a question, or a topic for students to think about followed by appropriate think time.

4. Lead students to have a partner or small group conversation about the topic.

5. After a few minutes, ask the students to pause their conversations and provide them with some conversation extenders to use with their partners. Examples include:

   "You said ______. Tell me more about that."

   "What did you mean when you said ______?"

   "I thought it was interesting when you said ______. I agree because …"

   "We both agree on ______. But we might disagree on …"

   "Where did you first hear/learn/see ______?"

■ Tips and Variations

♦ The goal is to have students use these types of questions and prompts naturally without having to be prompted. However, as is the case with any skill, it will take some practice and feedback before it becomes a habit.

♦ Depending on the age and needs of your students, consider creating a poster of conversation extenders or placing prompts on cards for students to access when having conversations.

♦ Deep, engaging conversations serve as a great experience to support writing tasks. Consider following up these conversations with a writing task that requires students to summarize, connect, and apply their thinking.

♦ **Differentiation Connection**: Different conversation extenders can be provided to students depending on their needs, language abilities, or interest level. In addition, some students might need to be prompted to talk more while others need to practice listening.

■ Overview

This strategy, intended for pairs or small groups, encourages students to make statements about their knowledge and finish each other's thoughts. Designed to deepen and extend conversations, students are required to build on the ideas of their partners.

■ Step by Step

1. Place students into pairs or small groups of no more than four students.

2. Designate a student to begin the conversation and tell the other students that they'll need to pay close attention to what is said because they'll be required to finish the thought.

3. Provide students with examples and model the process. For example, the first student might say something like, "The Colonial settlement at Williamsburg was important because …" The first student only begins the statement; they do not finish it. In this example, the first student would not tell why the settlement was important. That is the role of their partner or the next person in the group.

4. The next student then finishes the sentence adding their own thoughts and ideas. That student then continues the process by making the first part of another statement. For example, the second student might respond by saying, "The Colonial settlement at Williamsburg was important because it served as the capital of the colony of Virginia for almost 100 years. Today, we can visit Williamsburg and see …"

5. The original student or the next student in the group then finishes that thought and adds another.

6. Roam the room and provide feedback and direction to students as they have their conversations. Encourage students to use books, resources, or other materials to support their conversations.

■ Tips and Variations

♦ As a follow-up to the conversations, consider asking students to write a summary to help deepen their learning.

♦ Most students will benefit from being given time to think about and pre-create statements. Provide them with time to create their statements using any available resources but remind students that they'll need to know the answers (or possible answers) as well.

♦ **Differentiation Connection**: Some students will benefit from pre-created statements provided to them. In this case, provide them on strips of paper or note cards. In some cases, students will need both the beginning statement as well as the answer and possible responses.

■ Overview

Brainstorming is often used in classrooms as a method to increase discussion and dialogue. However, brainstorming sessions often reduce the amount of genuine discussion among students once a few students have offered ideas or suggestions. This strategy calls the order of the brainstorming session to be reversed.

■ Step by Step

1. Tell students that they'll be given a chance to brainstorm ideas and topics related to the objective of the lesson. If needed, have a brief discussion with students about their knowledge of brainstorming.

2. Remind students of the focus of the lesson or unit.

3. Tell students that a traditional brainstorming session starts with the whole group. That is, the leader/teacher selects a topic and everyone in the whole group offers ideas and suggestions. Once the whole group agrees upon some ideas or action items, small groups or individuals then act upon those ideas. In other words, brainstorming sessions usually begin with the whole group and end with individuals carrying out tasks or completing jobs. However, we are going to flip the brainstorm and start with some individual work before we talk as a whole group.

4. Give students a topic and provide them some time to *individually* brainstorm, write, or list ideas and applications.

5. Once students have individually brainstormed, ask them to share their ideas with partners or small groups. This will allow students a chance to get feedback, verbally clarify their ideas, and look for commonalities.

6. Once partners or small groups have discussed their ideas, lead a whole group discussion on the topic.

■ Tips and Variations

♦ The true power of flipping the brainstorm is that it offers students a chance to come up with their own ideas prior to being influenced by others. Furthermore, sharing their ideas in the safety of partners or small groups allows them to clarify, elaborate, and deepen their ideas.

■ Overview

Intended as a quick way to jump-start student conversations, this strategy requires the teacher to jumble—or mix up—words and phrases that are essential to the learning objective. Students are then tasked with working together to correct the jumble.

■ Step by Step

1. Prior to the lesson, create two to three phrases or sentences that summarize essential learning or that contain key facts and concepts that students must remember. For example, when studying the concept of median in math, display the following words for students—*middle, the, in, list, of, value, is, median, the, numbers, a.* (Answer: The median is the middle value in a list of numbers.)

2. Tell students that they'll be given a jumbled, or mixed up, list of words and that their job is to work with their partners to create a complete sentence using all the words from the list.

3. Remind students of the focus of the lesson along with the term or concept they'll be discussing. In the example above, you might say:

   Students, we have been studying the concepts of mean, median, and mode. For the next few minutes, we'll be focusing our discussions on median. Take a moment to think about what you know about median. Now, take a look at the board. I've listed 11 words that can be used to define the term median. Take the next 2–3 minutes and work with your partners to create a complete sentence using all those words.

4. Display the words and prompt students to begin working with their partners.

■ Tips and Variations

♦ Solving the jumbled summary is not the end, it is the means to an end. As an academic talk strategy, the goal is to get students to discuss the content with each other.

♦ Depending on the number of words in the jumble, there may be more than one correct answer.

♦ **Differentiation Connection:** One option is to include two to three words in the jumble that do not belong. In the example in Step 1, you might include the words mean and mode. In this case, inform the students that there are a couple of words that should not be used.

♦ **Technology Connection:** Utilize an interactive whiteboard or an app that allows you to create interactive activities to create a digital version to sort into a summary. Depending on the app, words can also be color coded by students to further sort vocabulary or other important terminology in the summary. Try the Word Mover at www.readwritethink.org or Lino at www.linoit.com.

■ Overview

During academic conversations, many students benefit from being provided specific terms or vocabulary words to use during their discussions. This strategy prompts students with the exact words, phrases, terms, or expressions that you want them to incorporate into their conversation.

■ Step by Step

1. Remind students of the objectives of the lesson or unit.

2. Provide students some time to review their notes, resources, or classwork, with the goal of coming to an understanding of their own knowledge of the topic.

3. Tell students that they'll be given some time to have a brief conversation with their peers about the focus of the lesson. However, tell students that you want them to use some specific words and terms during their conversations. For example, you might say, "Students, you'll be provided with about 3 minutes to have a partner conversation about the role appeasement played in World War II. During your conversations, I want you to use the following terms: policy, concessions, conflict, Germany, and Britain."

4. Display the selected words so all students can refer to them during their discussions.

5. During student conversations, move around the room listening to student conversations and providing feedback where needed.

6. If appropriate, debrief with the class.

■ Tips and Variations

♦ Key word lists are often combined with the use of Sentence Starters. For example, ask students to use the terms *convert*, *numerator*, and *simplify* when completing a sentence such as, "I came to the answer by …"

♦ This approach is an excellent tool for informal assessment. When students are required to verbalize what they know about a topic, errors in thinking become obvious. Likewise, students who truly understand a topic are more likely to be able to explain it clearly.

♦ Depending on the needs of your students, consider asking them to do a brief writing activity prior to their conversations. This will provide some students the necessary time to clarify their thoughts and create a coherent response.

♦ **Technology Connection:** Pair this activity with *Backchannel* or *Collaborative Sticky Notes* to allow students to post their sentences after the discussions.

■ Overview

There is a wide body of evidence that suggests that the use of nonverbal communication—including gesturing—has a significant impact on what we think and remember. Gesturing is a surprisingly simple and powerful way to communicate important messages. When gestures are used during discussions, students will be more engaged and have a clearer understanding of important ideas (Katja et al., 2015).

■ Step by Step

1. Give students time to think about the major events, concepts, or ideas in your current lesson or unit of study.

2. Tell students that you will be giving them time to talk about what they have been learning, but that you'll be adding a unique twist to their conversations.

3. Pose a question or give students a prompt related to the objective and have them participate in small group discussions.

4. After a few minutes, pause the discussions and say something like, "Now is the time for the twist. In just a moment, you are going to continue your small group discussions but you have to add a hand gesture or a series of gestures during your conversation."

5. Explain to students the rationale and purpose for the gestures. If appropriate, tell students about the power of nonverbal communication and provide some real-world examples of how we all communicate verbally and nonverbally with things like hand motions and facial expressions.

6. Provide some models or examples to students showing how they can communicate an idea or concept both verbally and nonverbally.

7. Place the students back into their small groups to continue their discussions making sure to monitor that students are attempting to add gestures.

■ Tips and Variations

♦ Perhaps the most universally understood gesture in the world involves the middle finger. Some students, particularly older ones, may try to mock this process or sneak in a couple of inappropriate gestures. It is important to know your students and provide clear expectations and directions.

♦ Remember to provide clear models and examples of gestures that students could use during their gesturing conversations.

♦ There are clear connections to vocabulary development and many teachers use gestures as a vocabulary strategy. While that is certainly appropriate, ensure that students discuss and talk about vocabulary in addition to just reading and writing about it.

♦ **Technology Connection:** Use technology to video record often-used gestures, especially those tied to key vocabulary terms that may be used throughout a unit or school year. QR codes can be added to a word wall and scanned to remind students of the gestures.

■ Overview

After a reading, a classroom discussion, or a project, this strategy challenges students to choose a position on a topic to defend their thoughts. After students "take a stance" they are then asked to "change your hat" to consider the perspectives and ideas of other individuals.

■ Step by Step

1. Remind students of the objectives, goals, and major outcomes of the assignment or unit you have been studying.

2. Ask students to take a stance, a position, or a viewpoint on a topic related to the lesson. For example, when studying issues related to the freedom of speech, ask students to take a defensible position on the issue of free speech in a school system. Pose a question such as, "Should there be limits on what students can say about their school, their teachers, or the school administration during non-school hours?"

3. Provide students with time to think about their answers and/or provide them with a short article or handout that provides some background or points to consider.

4. Place students in small groups and ask them to share their answers and their opinions with their peers.

5. After a few minutes, ask students to pause their conversations and then prompt them to "change their hats." In this scenario, a "hat" is a responsibility, title, position, or perspective that an individual assumes. During the previous discussion, most students were answering the question from a student's point of view. When they change hats, they are being asked to consider the same issue from someone else's viewpoint. Say something like, "Students, we are going to go deeper into this issue, but I am going to challenge you to think about the issue of free speech from a different perspective. Think about this for a moment, would you have that same perspective or belief if you were a school principal?"

6. Provide students with time to think about their responses from this new perspective.

7. After a few minutes, have them share with their small groups or lead a whole group discussion.

■ Tips and Variations

♦ Remember not to skip on the think time/wait time during this strategy. This is particularly necessary when students are asked to change hats.

♦ It may be necessary, if students seem to get stuck when considering another hat/perspective, to prepare some "what if" questions or other prompts to get students to consider other points of view.

♦ This strategy meshes well with many of the strategies described in the writing section of this book. In fact, depending on the needs of your students, you may elect to have them write their ideas prior to the small group discussions.

■ Overview

When viewing videos, video clips, or movies, turn on the captions. This simple trick increases student engagement, comprehension, and long-term memory (Collins, 2013). The captions encourage students to focus on specific information and increases the amount of sensory data the brain is asked to process.

■ Step by Step

1. Prior to showing the video, remind students of the objective of the lesson or unit, and explain the purpose of the video and what it is you want students to look for or think about while viewing it.

2. Explain to students that the video will have the captions turned on and why you chose to do that. If helpful, tell students that when they read and hear information at the same time, their brains will be processing (and remembering) more of the information.

3. Show the video.

4. Pause the video at predetermined times to pose questions or have the students respond in writing to what they are learning.

5. After the video is over, ask students to process what they have learned or what questions they have about the content in the video.

■ Tips and Variations

♦ Depending on the age or instructional needs of your students, you may elect not to tell them why the captions are turned on. In this way, you could conduct a small experiment to see if students notice and what they say about having them turned on.

♦ While most students love to watch movies or videos, they often equate "movie time" to non-learning time. Because of this, it is essential to always connect the video or movie to the instructional objective and to be explicit about what you want students to learn.

♦ **Differentiation Connection**: When pausing the video, challenge students to pose their own questions or to consider the major ideas or points that were just highlighted in the video. For example, say, "Students, at this point of the video, I am not going to ask a question or tell you what I think is important. Instead, I want you to think about what was just highlighted in the video and pose a question or make a statement of your own."

♦ **Technology Connection**: Many online videos include captions as well. Look for the ability to turn on these captions within the video player that you are utilizing.

Part Two

Energizers

Key Idea: *Energizers are brief movement-based strategies that allow students to step away from formal focused learning activities in order to re-energize and have fun. Each strategy typically takes less than 5 minutes but pays off with increased focus and attention once students resume the formal learning activity.*

Cambridge University neuroscientist Daniel Wolpert has spent years researching one seemingly simple question, *Why do we have brains?* On the surface the answer seems rather obvious—to allow us to communicate with the world around us, to think and create memories, or to build civilizations and culture. In his popular TED talk video, he explains that those reasons are completely wrong. In fact, he says, we have brains for *only one reason*—to coordinate and direct physical movement through our environment. In other words, we have brains because we have bodies that move around in our environment.

To prove his point, he asks us to consider the natural world. In nature, only those things that move require a brain. If something doesn't move, it has no need for a brain. Take a potted plant, for example. It has no brain *because* it is not required to move in its environment. While it does grow, it does not move of its own accord. Aardvarks, ants, birds, and people all move. Thus, the need for a brain. That is why brains exist—to facilitate movement in the world. While our brains do a lot more than merely coordinate the contractions of muscles, it seems that movement is central to brain function.

As you consider how to incorporate movement-based energizers into your classroom, consider some of what we know about the power of physical movement as it relates to learning, memory, and behavior:

- Dr John Ratey, in his popular 2008 book *Spark*, points out that exercise and movement impacts learning by improving alertness and attention.

- Although it can be an expensive alternative, some schools have begun providing standing desks to their students. A 2015 study found an average 12 percent increase in on-task behavior for students who used standing desks. That equated to about 7 minutes more attention per hour (Dornhecker et al., 2015).

- In 2015, researchers at the University of Central Florida found that movement opportunities improved outcomes and learning for students diagnosed with attention deficit hyperactivity disorder (ADHD). Dr Mark Rapport, one of the study's authors, stated, "The message isn't 'Let them run around the room.' But you need to be able to facilitate their movement so they can maintain the level of alertness necessary for cognitive activities." In an earlier 2009 study, Dr Rapport found that ADHD students fidgeted the most when they were trying to focus and pay attention.

- Students who are more physically fit get better grades in school (Coe et al., 2006).

- Twelve minutes of running in place increases students' attention and reading comprehension (Tine, 2014).

- Students who are more aerobically fit have more white matter—a substance in the brain associated with the efficient functioning of nerve cells (Chaddock-Heyman et al., 2014).

◆ Too much sitting and "downtime" is associated with higher levels of anxiety (Teychenne, 2015).

◆ Brief rest breaks after reading improves memory and recall (Dewar et al., 2012).

◆ The cerebellum, the part of the brain that coordinates movement, is also involved in executive functions such as attention, long-term memory, and impulse control (Bellebaum & Daum, 2007).

◆ Activities labeled as fun increase motivation and academic performance for students who typically underperform academically (Hart & Albarracin, 2009).

In an insightful 2015 article, Carolina Blatt-Gross, a professor from Gwinnet College, pondered the question of movement in the classroom and wrote:

> The paradigm of the still, quiet classroom with neatly aligned desks unfortunately requires that some students spend a great deal of energy complying with physical restrictions rather than learning. Certainly, at some point children need to learn to control their bodies. But making it an overriding concern in the classroom might be a waste.

Some educators spend so much time trying to restrict movement, they don't realize that movement may in fact be a solution to many of the challenges they face with their students.

While we want educators to make wise decisions about the use of instructional time, it is important to understand that the expectation of long periods of constant attention and focus is counterproductive. The brain and the body need breaks. The strategies we describe in this section provide easy-to-use, fun, and engaging brain breaks for students of all ages. We have specifically included strategies that do not require a lot of preparation or materials to be utilized. It is also important to note that energizers are not solely for younger students who still want to "play games." Students of all ages, including adults, will experience benefits from these short, divergent activities.

Quite simply, spending long periods of time in a still, sedentary state is incompatible with effective brain functioning. Our brains were designed to move and physical movement impacts cognition, attention, memory, and behavior. In fact, the topic of a sedentary lifestyle was addressed by Dr James Levine from the Mayo Clinic in Arizona. He said, "Sitting is more dangerous than smoking," and that we are "sitting ourselves to death."

One objection we occasionally hear is "We don't have time for these 'fun' energizer activities." Sometimes the word "fun" is used as a pejorative, as if true learning and fun are unable to coexist. Setting aside the research that shows a correlation between movement, fun, and learning, let's consider the approach many schools have taken over the last decade: reducing or outright eliminating physical education and recess to increase instructional time. Have we seen large, across-the-board benefits in student achievement as a result of limiting student activity? While there may be pockets of success and anecdotal stories, the research shows the opposite is true. The more we restrict movement—the more we try to get kids to be sedentary and still—the worse it is for their social, emotional, and cognitive development, and there is compelling evidence that movement helps to increase academic performance (Jarrett, 2013). If you want to increase student achievement, one of the best things you can do is increase physical activity.

As the name implies, the strategies we offer here will energize students so they will be more likely to focus, pay attention, and complete academic tasks after they participate in these activities.

■ Overview

This energizer requires one small, easily catchable ball and between 2–4 minutes for maximum effectiveness. Just as the name implies, this game involves the students tossing a ball to each other.

■ Step by Step

1. Prior to the game, locate a small ball that is soft and easily catchable.

2. The rules of the game are simple: start with a selected student and prompt him or her to toss the ball to another student in the room. When that student catches the ball (or retrieves the ball in case they did not catch it), they toss the ball to another student. Each student must toss the ball to a student who has not yet had the ball. If the ball is not caught by the student who is the intended target, it is their responsibility or choice to get the ball themselves or ask for help retrieving it.

3. Explain the rules of the game and ensure that students understand the difference between *throwing* the ball and *tossing* the ball. A toss is underhand, while a throw is overhand. A toss typically has an arch to the trajectory, while a throw is in more of a straight line. A toss is easy to catch, while a throw is difficult to catch. Model the difference for students and explain the need to stay within the rules of the game.

4. Have students stand or sit on their desks to begin the game.

5. Begin the game.

6. End the game when all students have had a chance to catch the ball.

■ Tips and Variations

♦ Although there is tremendous value in providing short, nonacademic breaks during class, some teachers prefer to have an academic connection to the game. In this case, the teacher could ask each student a review question prior to tossing the ball.

♦ To help students remember who has caught the ball and who has not, you could ask students to sit after they have caught and tossed the ball.

♦ Some teachers prefer to use a silent version of this game—sometimes called "Quiet Ball." In this case, students are not able to verbalize, talk, request the ball, or make any comments during the game.

■ Overview

How Many Can You Name is a classic brainstorming game where students are given a category and asked to name, compile, list, or brainstorm as many answers as they can to a specific question.

■ Step by Step

1. Prior to the game, think of general categories or topics that are of high interest to your students. Topics could include things like flavors of ice cream, superheroes, animals, famous people, or movies.

2. Create several sentence stems such as *Types of…*; *Things that are …*; and *Kinds of…* for use with the categories. For example, you might tell students to brainstorm as many flavors of ice cream as they can or to think of things that are slimy.

3. Use the sentence stems to challenge your students, either alone or in small groups, to brainstorm as many answers that fit the category as they can.

4. Depending on the age and format of your classroom, give your students a time limit from 1 to 3 minutes.

5. After the time limit, have students share their lists.

■ Tips and Variations

♦ This strategy provides a great opportunity to be creative, unique, and a little bit goofy. You could ask students to generate answers to categories like, *Things that are sparkly, Things that get washed,* or *Things that break easily.*

♦ Students love creating their own categories and topics.

♦ Although this is not an academic strategy, it can easily be used to support vocabulary development and writing skills. For example, if you ask your students to brainstorm a list of *Things that talk* to help them develop story lines, dialogue, and story elements.

♦ As you play this game several times, consider keeping track of the categories and compiling them into a master list or assembled on note cards for future use. As students brainstorm additional ideas, they can be added to the master list.

■ Overview

The statements made during the *Imagine That* energizer challenge students to briefly act out a scenario that is described by the teacher.

■ Step by Step

1. Prior to the use of this strategy, create, collect, or compile a list of age appropriate and relevant statements that your students will find funny, silly, engaging, or challenging. All the statements must include the phrase "Imagine that" and require the students to act out how they imagine the phrase would look. Examples include:

   "Imagine that you are an elephant trying to drink a can of soda."

   "Imagine that you are a 5-year-old learning to ride a bike for the first time."

   "Imagine that there is an old person who hears rap music for the first time."

   "Imagine that a robot is trying to learn the Running Man (dance move)."

   "Imagine that two people are trying to sit in a chair at the same time."

2. Ask the students to stand up.
3. Make the *Imagine That* statement and prompt your students to act it out.
4. Repeat with additional statements as needed to energize the class.

■ Tips and Variations

♦ As with some of the other energizer strategies and topics, students will be good sources of *Imagine That* statements. However, it is always a good idea to vet those statements before giving them to the whole class.

♦ While a direct academic connection is not necessary, this strategy could provide some excellent experiences for students to use as a basis for creative writing assignments.

■ Overview

This strategy is extremely simple but results in increased energy, focus, and alertness, and allows students to experience the connection between the brain and the body.

■ Step by Step

1. Begin by telling students about the connections between the body and the brain. Say something like, "Students, did you know that what you do with your body has a direct impact on how you think, how you feel, and how much you learn? For example, you all know that your brain needs a healthy supply of oxygen to operate properly. Sitting for long periods of time slows down your metabolism and the amount of blood flowing to your brain. So, let's take a minute to get the blood flowing again." Elaborate as needed depending on the age or interest level of your students.

2. Ask students to stand up.

3. Lead students in about 30 seconds of deep breathing exercises making sure you are modeling and participating fully.

4. During or after deep breathing, lead your students in some stretching exercises. Ensure that all major muscle groups of the body are engaged.

■ Tips and Variations

♦ Deep breathing exercises also help to reduce stress. As a result, many teachers lead their students through deep breathing exercises before exams, tests, or presentations.

♦ Many teachers also lead the *Stand, Stretch, and Breathe* process prior to asking students to engage in partner activities, writing tasks, or discussions. This process helps to calm students and gives them an opportunity to think and reflect prior to engaging in an academic task.

♦ While some parents and communities are reluctant to fully adopt a yoga-based approach in schools, there is compelling research that demonstrates benefits for students and staff. One of our favorite resources is www.yogainschools.org.

■ Overview

This super simple strategy involves having students stand when they can answer, recognize, understand, or relate to a given prompt.

■ Step by Step

1. Prior to the lesson, prepare a list of prompts that are relevant, funny, or interesting to your students. For example, your prompts might include:

   "Stand when you can describe the taste of Brussels sprouts."

   "Stand when you can recall the last time you tried to run backwards."

   "Stand when you can name three characters from Star Wars."

   "Stand when you can say three things you'd do if you had $1000."

   "Stand when you can name something that glows in the dark."

2. Tell students that you'll be making some statements and that you want them to think about their response and then stand when they have an answer.

3. Tell students that just because they stand up it does not mean that they'll be required to share their answer.

4. Say a prompt and allow students time to think about their answers.

5. If appropriate, have students share their answers or ideas with their peers.

6. Repeat with as many *Stand When* prompts as necessary to energize the group.

■ Tips and Variations

♦ The goal of this strategy is to get students out of their seats and thinking about a specific prompt or question. Therefore, select prompts or questions that have mass appeal that will result in most of your students standing at some point during the strategy.

♦ While no clear academic connection needs to be made for this strategy, it is simple to add prompts and questions that focus on the objectives of a lesson. For example, when studying the solar system, you could say, "Stand when you can name one difference between a planet and a star."

♦ Note that the strategy is titled *Stand When*, not *Stand If*. The goal is to get students to stand and the use of the term *when* implies that all students will be able to participate. The use of the word if offers students the chance to opt out.

♦ For additional *Stand When* prompts, challenge your students to create their own original ideas.

■ Overview

This sometimes-silly energizer challenges students to strike a pose according to a title or category they are given.

■ Step by Step

1. Prior to using this energizer, spend a few minutes gathering examples of famous postures or poses. Examples might include:

   The Statue of Liberty

   Thinking Man

   Wonder Woman

   The Dab

   Usain Bolt

   The kid from the *Home Alone* movie.

2. Before the energizer, tell students that a "pose" is a particular way of standing, sitting, or a body position. Model a couple of examples and/or provide images and pictures of famous poses. For example, you might say, "Students, in just a moment I am going to challenge you to copy, as best you can, the posture or pose of someone or something famous."

3. Show students a few examples and ask them to show their best pose, copying the model as best they can. For those students who are unfamiliar with the pose, have them copy their neighbors.

4. Repeat the process and give students a chance to do several different poses.

5. As students become better and better at striking a pose, consider combining two different poses. For example, you might ask students to show the stance of what it would look like if someone was crossing the finish line of a race while playing the air guitar.

■ Tips and Variations

♦ Poses or postures do not have to be solely from famous examples. One alternative is to describe an emotion or a physical condition and have students replicate what you describe. For example, you might ask students to strike a pose of someone who is in the starting blocks for the 100-meter dash, about to sneeze, yawning, or frightened.

♦ Students are a great source of ideas for this energizer. However, depending on the age and maturity level of your students, it is a good idea to have students tell you their ideas before they are presented in front of the entire class.

♦ For additional ideas, do an internet search for emojis.

■ Overview

This strategy tests students' observation and recall skills by asking them to study a group of items placed on a table.

■ Step by Step

1. Prior to the use of this energizer, select between 15 and 20 common classroom items and place them in a bag or a container. Selected items could include things like a stapler, a pencil sharpener, a Post-it note, keys, and so on. All the items should be easily identifiable by students; do not select any items that students are unfamiliar with.

2. Take the items from the bag and spread them out on a table, ensuring that students cannot see the items while this is happening. Cover up the items with a towel or a small blanket.

3. Ask the students to stand around the table, making sure the items are still covered.

4. Tell the students that they will have 1 minute to look at and study the items on the table and that their goal is to remember as many of the items as possible.

5. Uncover the items and start the timer.

6. After 1 minute, cover the items back up and ask students to go back to their seats and write a list of as many items as they can remember.

7. After the students have written their lists, uncover the items again and have students compare the actual items to the lists they wrote.

■ Tips and Variations

♦ While this strategy is designed as a fun energizer, it provides a great opportunity to talk with students about concepts related to working memory. Most notably, working memory can be strengthened with games that challenge us to recall items from a list.

♦ It is possible (although less impactful) to do this strategy with an image of 20 objects instead of having them placed on a table. In this case, ensure that the image is projected large enough so students can easily identify all of the items. It is also important to select items that are large enough that they'll be clear in the photo.

♦ Depending on the needs of the students in your classroom, this could be a partner activity. In that case, after students have created their lists from memory (Step 6), have them compare their lists with partners.

♦ Like all the strategies listed in the Energizers section, there is no need to provide students with points, rewards, or privileges if they do well on this task. The goal is for students to participate in a short, divergent activity to energize them so they can use that energy when asked to focus back on an instructional task.

■ Overview

This classic children's game energizes students because it includes elements of social interaction, physical movement, novelty, and humor. While no direct academic connection is necessary, it is simple to include key concepts, vocabulary, or topics related to the instructional objectives.

■ Step by Step

1. Ask students to form a circle. If a circle formation is not possible due to the classroom setup, students can form two lines facing each other. The formation can be either sitting or standing.

2. Choose a phrase, a series of key words, or a short sentence and whisper it to a student who will start the game. For added impact, write the phrase on a slip of paper so students can see it at the end of the game. Tell students that their job is to listen to the phrase carefully because they'll need to repeat it exactly as they hear it.

3. The first student then whispers the phrase to the student next to them doing their best to repeat it exactly as they heard it.

4. This process is repeated until all students have participated by both listening to and repeating the phrase.

5. The last student then says the phrase aloud so the entire class can hear it.

■ Tips and Variations

♦ A common question is, "What if I have a student who purposefully sabotages the game?" In that case, there are a couple of options. First, it is always important to remember the needs and unique characteristics of your class. If a student cannot participate appropriately in the game, they'll need to opt out. However, consider allowing them to be the very first person who starts the game and ask them to read the phrase directly from a sheet of paper or note card.

♦ **Critical Thinking Connection:** This game offers an excellent opportunity to discuss topics such as the art of listening, short term memory, and personal bias.

■ Overview

With very little prep time required, it doesn't get much more simple than the "Or" game. This strategy challenges students to make a choice based on an "or" statement.

■ Step by Step

1. Prior to the game, brainstorm topics, categories, or issues that have two clear options. For example, you might ask the students to select their favorite: Coke or Pepsi, PCs or Macs, Star Wars or Star Trek, Pirates or Ninjas, and so on.

2. Make a statement and ask students to select their choice, reminding them that the only rule is that they must make a choice between the two.

3. Students can signal their choice by a show of hands, by standing, or by saying aloud which choice they select.

4. If appropriate, have students share their choices with partners or small groups and have students explain or elaborate on their choices.

■ Tips and Variations

♦ In the example given in step 1 (Coke or Pepsi), it is inevitable that a student will say, "I don't like either, I like Dr Pepper." In this case, simply remind students that you are asking them to choose one of the two and that they don't necessarily need to like both of them. In this case, it is a bit like the popular *Would You Rather* game. Students simply need to make a choice.

♦ With this strategy, you can get very creative and students love to come up with their own "or" statements.

♦ Consider compiling a master list of "or" statements and posting it in the classroom.

♦ While this is not designed as an academic strategy, consider reinforcing academic talk skills such as elaboration, questioning, and paraphrasing as students share their choices with each other.

■ Overview

This quick energizer is a unique variation on the classic game of hide-and-seek, where one student attempts to discover which of their classmates has left the classroom.

■ Step by Step

1. Select a student to begin the game. This student is asked to leave the classroom.

2. While that student is out of earshot, and cannot see into the classroom, select another student to also leave the classroom but they need to exit via a different door than the first student.

3. Ask the first student to reenter the classroom and give them a specified amount of time (10–15 seconds) to look around the room and then guess or name the student who is missing. Depending on the age of the students, the child may get more than one guess.

4. As time permits, repeat this process with other students.

■ Tips and Variations

♦ If the classroom setup does not allow for two different students to leave via different doors, select two students to change seats. The student who was waiting outside then names the students who switched seats. In this case, the game becomes *Who's Moved?*

♦ Some students prefer to team up for this game. In a team-oriented variation, groups of two to three students are asked to leave the classroom (Step 1) to guess *Who's Missing?*

♦ Another variation involves changing certain (fairly obvious) elements of the classroom environment. For example, while the selected student is waiting outside, consider turning a chair upside-down, placing a goofy hat on a student, or have all the students cross their arms. This variation then becomes a game of *What's Changed?*

Part Three

Feedback

Key Idea: *Authentic, personalized, and timely feedback is among the most powerful tools teachers have to engage students in meaningful learning. Not only is feedback extremely effective at increasing student achievement, all students crave authentic feedback about their status, progress, and growth. Effective feedback always leads to learning.*

As a method to engage students and increase achievement, feedback has been studied intently over the last 30 years. As a result, just about any discussion about how to increase student achievement will inevitably include talk about feedback. But, what exactly is feedback and why does it matter in terms of engagement and learning? How does feedback differ from praise, criticism, or advice and what are some of the most powerful strategies for increasing the quantity and quality of the feedback we provide to students?

We'll address all those questions and more, but let's start with a workable, classroom-based definition for feedback: *Feedback is actionable information about a task, process, behavior, or product that is provided in a timely manner so that students have evidence or data upon which to make a decision.* While some authors and researchers will emphasize different aspects or characteristics of feedback, there are several common features of effective feedback. Culled from the research of educators like Marzano, Jensen, Hattie, Brookhart, Wiliam, and Wiggins, here are some commonly agreed-upon guidelines for the effective use of feedback in the classroom:

- It is prompt and timely rather than delayed.
- It is specific rather than general.
- It focuses on a task or characteristic of the work rather than the personal qualities of the individual.
- It is specific to an individual rather than generalized to a group.
- It is simplified rather than complex.
- It is low-stakes rather than high-stakes.
- It is often rather than rare.
- It comes from a trusted source.
- It must result in some change on the part of the recipient.
- It should build effort and encouragement rather than discouragement.
- It is focused on a learning goal.

John Hattie, in his groundbreaking book entitled *Visible Learning* (2009), found that feedback had an effect size of 0.73. An effect size is used by researchers to indicate how significant an approach or strategy is in terms of student growth and achievement. Hattie refers to anything over a 0.4 as being in the "zone of desired effects." In other words, with a 0.73 effect size, the effective use of feedback can be expected to show significant results for students. While statistics, sampling, and effect sizes may not get you excited, what you need to know is this—feedback is extremely powerful and among the most effective things you can implement in your classroom. In fact, Hattie lists feedback as one of his top ten high-impact strategies to accelerate student growth. Hattie goes on to state that feedback answers three basic but critical questions every learner needs to wrestle with to cement long-term learning: *Where am I going? How am I going?* and *Where to next?*

Tracey Tokuhama-Espinosa, a leader in the Mind-Brain-Education movement, approaches the concept of feedback from the perspective of what happens in the brain when students receive feedback. She says, "feedback is based on the premise that in order to improve learning, students need to know what they do not yet know (where they have erred)." She goes on to highlight that this knowledge is only the first step. Once students know what they do not know, they need to be given explicit instruction on how to correct their errors in order to improve future performance (Tokuhama-Espinosa, 2011). A key idea here is that feedback is always preceded by and followed by instruction.

It is not enough to provide students with actionable information; we must also provide them with instruction, direction, and guidance on how to improve in the future. This, by the way, is a significant reason that grades often fall short in terms of providing effective feedback to students. A grade or percentage provided on an assignment is often not actionable. While it may be accurate and relevant information, if there is nothing students can do with the grade, it is not feedback. If teachers do not provide information and instruction about how to improve or adjust for future assignments, the data becomes dead and static. Feedback provides evidence about a student's status (where they might be right, where they might be wrong, etc.) as well as how to improve. Again, effective feedback is always preceded *and* followed by instruction. Assessment guru Dylan Wiliam (2016) reminds educators that "Feedback is only successful if students use it to improve their performance." If there is no instruction on the part of the teacher and no action taken on the part of the student, it is not feedback.

When designing effective feedback strategies and protocols in the classroom, there are a few concepts that are sometimes confused with authentic, research-based feedback. Grant Wiggins, perhaps most well-known for co-authoring *Understanding by Design* with Jay McTighe (2005), reminded teachers that there are significant differences between feedback, praise, and advice. Feedback is actionable information about what a person did or did not do. It is merely a description of the traits of a performance, the outcome of a task, or status of a process. Advice is what a learner might do to honor the feedback and improve their performance. A problem arises when educators confuse the two. While giving advice does play a role in learning, it should come after the student has received feedback, if it is needed at all. Like advice, praise can also play a role in learning, but it is not synonymous with feedback.

As an example, imagine your students are working on a writing assignment and you want to provide feedback about their progress. True feedback sounds like this: "Allie, I can see that you used a graphic organizer to arrange your ideas before you began writing and that those ideas appear in your first draft." In this example, feedback is just a statement of fact. Too often teachers then throw a praise statement or a suggestion (advice) for students to consider. While praise and advice might be necessary under some circumstances, when teachers routinely use them instead of true feedback, the effectiveness is lost. In the above example, if the teacher followed up with "good job" or "great work" and then told the student to "Remember to go back and make sure all the ideas from your graphic organizer end up in your essay," the power of feedback is diluted. Advice tells a student what to do and does not require the student to think for themselves. The true power of feedback (defined as actionable information) is that it requires the students to act, think, comprehend, and decide. Merely telling students what to do via advice requires none of those things. Likewise, praise statements do not require the students to be actively engaged or thoughtful. Being on the receiving end of a praise statement might make students feel good temporarily, but it does not provide them with any information that they can act upon. Does this mean praise and advice are bad things?

No, of course not. There are times when students will need follow-up advice if they get stuck or a praise statement if they need a little motivation, but those things come only after feedback. They don't replace feedback. It is important to note here that praise and advice can be complimentary, but only feedback is correlated to achievement (Hattie, 2009).

With this background about feedback, we offer the following strategies to increase the quality and effectiveness of feedback in your classroom.

■ Overview

This strategy provides students the opportunity to discover, on their own, what knowledge they have developed and any gaps they might have in their learning.

■ Step by Step

1. Provide each student with a blank sheet of paper.

2. Tell them to list the alphabet—A to Z—down the side of the paper. To save time, some teachers opt to provide students with a pre-printed handout.

3. Prompt students to think about the major outcomes, learning, or knowledge they have developed during the current unit of study.

4. Tell students that they'll take a few minutes to complete the A to Z Brainstorm sheet by listing content, vocabulary terms, concepts, or examples that begin with the various letters of the alphabet. For example, when studying a unit on the major muscle groups of the body, a student might list deltoids next to the letter D or quadriceps next to the letter Q.

5. Give students time to complete their A to Z Brainstorm.

6. Once students complete their lists, lead a discussion or show them terms or concepts that you listed. During the discussion, challenge students to think about what items they may have missed and ask students to add concepts or terms to their original brainstorm.

7. Lead students to review the lists and evaluate the depth of their knowledge. Prompt them with statements such as, "What concepts or terms did you not include that you realize now are important?"

■ Tips and Variations

♦ Feedback that is self-discovered can be some of the most powerful learning available to students. During the process of using an A to Z Brainstorm, ensure that students have time to truly reflect upon the list with the goal of evaluating their own knowledge.

♦ The A to Z Brainstorm lists can serve as an excellent source of information for student-to-student discussion or for written summaries.

Overview

An "Anchor" is a concrete model, visual, artifact, or paper that shows students exactly what an end product might look like. In essence, an Anchor provides students with a target or an example to which they can compare their own work.

Step by Step

1. Prior to beginning a lesson or unit, locate exemplary samples of student work. In some cases, this might be a model of a project or a written work that shows students exactly what an outcome *might* look like. The goal is for students to get a sense of what success in the task or assignment is like.

2. Tell students the objective of the lesson or focus of the unit.

3. Show students the Anchors by saying something like, "Students, we are about to start a unit on the study of biomes. As part of our unit, we will be creating models and diagrams that show our knowledge of biomes. I have a couple of examples here to show you. These are examples of what your project might look like. Let's take a look and talk about these examples." Highlight the fact that these models are *mights*. That is, they show students what their end product might or could look like but that they should not simply copy it.

4. As students begin to create their own products or papers, prompt them to compare their own work against the Anchor.

Tips and Variations

- Recall that feedback does not need to come solely from the teacher. In fact, feedback doesn't even need to come from a person in order to be effective. Providing students with models and examples is an excellent way for them to reflect and give feedback to themselves.

- For students that are motivated by grades, the use of an Anchor provides a very clear path towards achievement.

- **Technology Connection**: While it isn't always possible to have a physical example in the room, use the internet to your advantage to look for images and examples that may be available online.

■ Overview

As a source of feedback, video and audio examples provide a tangible, reliable, and easily referenced source of information about one's progress.

■ Step by Step

1. Prior to starting a lesson or a unit, spend some time searching for examples of the skill that you want students to develop or exemplars of the product you wish students to develop.

2. At an appropriate time during the lesson, show students the examples you have collected. Explain their purpose and how they'll be used. Say something like, "Students, during our lesson today we are going to be taking a look at a couple of videos that show exactly what your end product might look like. These examples will provide you with a very clear source of information so that you can compare your work against what you see in the example."

3. At various points during the lesson(s), remind students to refer to the examples. Depending on the needs of your students, prompt them with questions or statements such as, "At this point in your project, go back and listen again to the audio example. Listen for how the speaker explained ..." or "What might our video example tell us about the next step in your project?"

■ Tips and Variations

♦ Another reason that audio and video examples are so powerful is because they do not change. As classroom teachers, our feedback can vary, even slightly, from day to day and from student to student. External, non-human sources of feedback provide a consistency of information that benefits students greatly.

♦ Make sure that the examples and models are easily accessible to students and remember to prompt students to refer to the examples at several points during the lesson or unit.

♦ **Differentiation Connection:** Depending on the skill or knowledge being developed by the students, different examples and models can be collected and shared with different groups of students.

■ Overview

Checklists can serve as excellent sources of feedback because they can prompt students to think about and take action on the exact steps they need to take in order to reach a target.

■ Step by Step

1. Prior to the lesson or unit, create a checklist that contains information about the process, the content, or the outcomes of the lesson.

2. At an appropriate time during the lesson, introduce students to the checklist(s) and explain their purpose. Say something like, "Students, I have created a checklist that we'll use during this project. The checklist shows us exactly what needs to be done and how it should be done. It will serve as a source of feedback and direction for us. We'll refer back to it several times during the unit in order to gauge our progress."

3. Hand out the checklists and lead students to review it, ask questions about it, and make plans for how to use it.

4. Throughout the lesson(s) or unit, prompt students to use their checklists in order to get a sense of their progress or learning. In this case, train students to view the checklist as more than a "to do" list; help them to view it as a source of information about what they are learning and what steps they need to take in order to meet the standards or expectations.

■ Tips and Variations

♦ There can be different types of checklists, depending on the needs of the students and the learning objective. Some teachers opt to focus initially on *component checklists*—those are lists that include the parts, sections, elements, or components that are required on a project. Those are helpful to ensure that students have all the necessary elements included in their project. However, *process checklists* can also be valuable. Those checklists outline *how* things are to be accomplished in addition to what needs to be accomplished.

♦ In addition to being an excellent source of feedback/actionable information, checklists also help to motivate students by helping them to see their progress. One of the great joys of using a checklist is the sense of accomplishment one feels when they are able to check something off the list.

♦ **Critical Thinking Connection**: Checklists can be a wonderful source of critical thinking for students when they are used to evaluate the *quality* of what is being completed. In this case, they can be similar to a rubric where students are required to think about and act upon specific quality components of their work.

■ Overview

One-on-one teacher and student conferencing is a powerful source of feedback and learning for students and teachers alike.

■ Step by Step

1. When planning, set aside time to have individual student conferences lasting between 3 and 5 minutes each.

2. When introducing the idea of a conference with your students, tell them that you will be taking time to meet individually with each of them so you can provide feedback and direction on their project, progress, or overall class performance.

3. Tell students about the format of the conference as well as the tasks they'll be completing while you meet individually with students.

4. One at a time, call students back to conduct the conference. Start by asking questions of the student to gauge their progress. Ask questions or make statements such as "How has your progress been so far?" or "What questions do you have about …" or "Show me something you are most proud of." Remember that, as a source of feedback, students should walk away from the conference with a clear understanding about actions they can or should take in order to improve or continue their learning.

■ Tips and Variations

♦ A true, authentic conference is two-sided. That is, students should not only listen to your guidance and feedback; they should also tell, ask questions, and share what they are learning. In this case, conferences can also be opportunities for students to demonstrate what they know or what they have learned.

♦ As a source of learning and feedback for teachers, reflect on the types of questions or issues that may arise from several student conferences. For example, if you hear the same questions from several students, it may indicate which topics or content needs to be retaught in a whole group setting.

♦ **Differentiation Connection**: Depending on the skill level of your students and the objective(s) of the lesson, students can conference with one another. In these cases, ensure that you provide a clear model for students to follow, including a script and questions to ask each other.

■ Overview

Too often in education, feedback is viewed as something that teachers provide *to* students via grades, verbal comments, or directions about behavior. In this case, the flow of information goes only from teacher to student. However, when teachers take time to get feedback *from* students, learning, relationships, and classroom culture all improve.

■ Step by Step

1. Take some time to think about the kind of feedback you want to collect from students. Do you want to know about activities or projects that were the most impactful? Do you want to know about your personal teaching skills such as clarity of directions or organization? Perhaps you want to know how students view grades in your classroom.

2. Create a quiz-type handout that lists questions and prompts along with some sort of rating scale. For example, your feedback form might include:

I provide clear directions	1 2 3 4 5
I provide enough time for you to complete your assignments	1 2 3 4 5
I take time to listen to student ideas	1 2 3 4 5
I am organized	1 2 3 4 5

3. Tell students about the course evaluation and how you intend to use the results. Say something like, "I want to take a few minutes to gather some feedback from you all. So, I have created a student to teacher feedback form where I want you to honestly rate my teaching ability and style. My goal is to simply get a better understanding of how I can improve my teaching. And, since you all spend every day with me, I want to hear what you have to say. You will not put your name on the handout, so you can be honest. When I collect all the forms, I'll put all the data together to see where I can improve."

4. Give students the evaluation.

5. Collect the evaluations and look at the data for trends and commonalities.

■ Tips and Variations

♦ In addition to providing statements that students can rate, you could also add open-ended questions. If this is done, make certain that students know that the results are only being used for your personal improvement and that you will not be compiling individual student results.

♦ Since the goal of a course evaluation is to gather feedback about teacher behavior, they should always be done anonymously by the students. In addition, the teacher should never use the feedback results for any sort of punishment or to make students feel guilty about how they rated the teacher.

♦ **Technology Connection:** Some teachers opt to use online survey websites such as Surveymonkey.com or Google Forms. Some teachers also opt to ask parents on to complete the evaluation.

■ Overview

Often used as a way to debrief tests or assessment, this strategy requires students to locate and correct errors in their work.

■ Step by Step

1. Prior to handing back student work, circle or highlight the places where students made mistakes. For example, when grading a math test, instead of marking an item correct or incorrect, simply circle an item to indicate that the student will need to follow up or revisit that question. Add a comment, question, or a statement such as, "Brody, the answer is wrong because you made an error in the second step when solving the problem. Try again paying close attention to that second step."

2. When handing back the assignment or test, tell students that they'll be spending some time reviewing their work with the goal of finding their mistakes and fixing them. Remind students that grades are important and they play a role in the class, but you are more interested in helping them see the mistakes they made and teaching them how to correct those mistakes.

3. Give students time to find and fix the mistakes in their assignment.

4. Roam the room and assist students in fixing their mistakes. Pay special attention to those students that cannot seem to fix their mistakes on their own. If appropriate, allow students to work in pairs or small groups to support each other.

■ Tips and Variations

♦ A major shortfall in the way we assess students is that we rarely review, revise, or revisit any of the content after the test. The *Teach-Test-Move On* approach is unfortunately way too common in classrooms. Students know that when a test is graded and handed back, they rarely have to think about those concepts again. However, if our goal is for students to remember the information, they have to understand why they made mistakes and how to correct them.

♦ Some teachers struggle with allowing students to correct mistakes in order to get a higher grade on an assignment. However, consider that the primary goal of teaching is not the assignment of grades. Our primary goal is to ensure that students learn and master the content. When students can revise and correct, they are more likely to master the content.

♦ It is important to recognize that this strategy will take time. However, merely covering a lot of content is not our goal. Our goal is to get students to deeply understand important information. Deep understanding takes time.

■ Overview

Most students, after considering the grade on a test, rarely go back to review the concepts or ideas that were tested. When we allow students to discard test results, we encourage rapid forgetting and reinforce a belief that the content and material is unimportant. This strategy requires students to review what they've learned (or what content they misunderstood) with the goal of learning and retaining important knowledge.

■ Step by Step

1. Prior to handing back student test or assessment results, prepare some age-appropriate questions, prompts, or topics for the students to reflect upon. Examples include:
   - Select two questions that you got right but were unsure about.
   - What question(s) did you get wrong that you thought you knew?
   - Did you leave any questions blank? Why?
   - How was your preparation for this test? Did that preparation impact the results?
   - Did you make any silly mistakes?
   - What part(s) were easiest? Most difficult?
   - Were there any questions or problems that you'd like to challenge?

2. Hand back student tests, assessments, or projects. Allow them some time to consider both the score/grade but also prompt them to look through the entire test examining which items they got correct and incorrect.

3. Lead the students to reflect upon the test results by saying something like, "Students, we know that tests allow us a chance to consider what we know and what we do not know about a topic. While grades are important, what we do after we get our scores back is very important. I've prepared a few questions and topics I want you to consider as you look through your test results."

4. Provide students with time to consider the questions and conduct their *Post-Test Review*.

5. Lead students to complete a written summary or ask them to share with partners.

■ Tips and Variations

- Similar to *Find and Fix*, this strategy tends to be a bit more reflective in nature because it requires students to think both about their knowledge as well as their performance on the assessment.

- Recall that authentic feedback is defined as "actionable information" for students. With this in mind, ensure that students are considering next steps with their knowledge. If appropriate, offer students a chance to retake the test.

- **Differentiation Connection**: What about a student who "aces" the test or gets a very high score? In those cases, offer the student an opportunity to reflect as much on the process of learning and studying as much as the content learned.

■ Overview

A brief quiz, assuming that students get immediate results, is a powerful and effective source of feedback. Because effective feedback should both identify and fill in gaps of knowledge for students, this approach helps students to get immediate information about their knowledge (or lack thereof).

■ Step by Step

1. Prior to the lesson, create a short quiz consisting of between three and five questions that are essential to the unit or lesson objectives.

2. Prompt students to take the quiz by saying something like, "Students, I want us to take a couple of minutes to get a handle on our understanding of the topics we've been studying. So, I've created a short five-question quiz. But, this quiz is designed to help you get a good understanding of what you know and what you may not know. Even though it's called a quiz, don't worry about the grade. The goal is for you to get some feedback about your knowledge. After you take the quiz, we are going to do something with the information."

3. Prompt students to take the quiz.

4. When all students have finished (or it's appropriate to move on), provide students with the answers to the questions.

5. Prompt students to consider more than just their "score" on the quiz. Lead students through the process of analyzing their results in order to answer questions such as: "What knowledge seems to be a strength?", What concepts or ideas need some more examples or elaboration?", or "What ideas are easiest to explain?".

■ Tips and Variations

♦ Grading and traditional summative assessment is not the goal of a *Quick Quiz*. Rather, the goal is to provide students an opportunity to test their own knowledge in a safe manner free of concern about a grade. As a feedback strategy, the goal is for students to get a clear picture of their knowledge along with any gaps or misunderstandings they may have.

♦ Since this strategy is not grade-centric, there is no need to try to "stump" students. Rather, after students take the quiz and consider the results, they should be more aware of their knowledge and any steps they may need to take to correct any misunderstandings.

♦ **Differentiation Connection**: Some students, as they are looking over the results of their quiz, will struggle to determine gaps in knowledge or next steps. In those cases, consider re-teaching concepts to students in small groups.

♦ **Technology Connection**: Consider pairing this strategy with *Clickers without Clickers*. Make sure the program you are using will give students individual feedback, as they will need it to complete Step 5. The advantage of this pairing is that you can also see all the individual student responses in order to monitor and adjust your instruction for the day's lesson.

Ticket in the Door

■ Overview

A very popular end-of-class strategy is the "Ticket out the Door" (sometimes called an "Exit Ticket") that requires students to summarize their knowledge or make a statement about something they learned during the lesson. "The Ticket *in* The Door" strategy is used to provide feedback to students as they enter the class.

■ Step by Step

1. Prior to class, collect and review work the students have previously produced. This could be a Ticket out the Door from a previous day, a journal entry, or an assessment.

2. Provide feedback on each student's work making sure to include specific points or questions for the students to consider. Remember that true feedback is defined as *actionable information* so students must be tasked with something specific to do with the feedback they receive.

3. As students enter the class, provide them with their Ticket in the Door and prompt them to read and respond to the feedback you have provided.

4. Walk around the room to ensure that students are responding to your feedback and answer questions or provide additional prompts for students to consider.

■ Tips and Variations

♦ This strategy will be most powerful when students are given substantive and specific responses to their work. General praise statements such as "Good Work" or "That's an excellent point you made" are not feedback and do not require the students to do anything with the praise they receive.

♦ This strategy can provide information about how to regroup students for re-teaching or enrichment opportunities.

♦ Some teachers elect to use *Response Journals* as a Ticket in the Door to prompt ongoing conversations with students about their learning.

Part Four

Questioning

Key Idea: *Asking questions is at the very heart of what we do as teachers and the role of teacher-as-questioner is as old as the profession itself. However, not all questioning strategies and techniques are created equally when it comes to engaging students in meaningful ways. Thoughtfully crafted questions employed with well-designed strategies engage students and lead to deeper, more long-term learning.*

Perhaps more has been written, said, and researched about questioning in the classroom than any other instructional method. In fact, questioning is so ubiquitous that no one challenges the notion that teachers should ask questions and students should answer them. While we certainly won't contest the fact that questions are at the very heart of learning, we will ask educators to reflect on the idea that questions alone don't necessarily lead to meaningful learning. Meaningful learning results when students are engaged in appropriate activities aligned to their interests and needs along with core learning objectives.

Rather than provide a primer or a research overview as we do in other chapters, here we offer a specific framework and a description of effective questioning characteristics that will build the foundation for the use of the ten specific strategies that are included. For those who would like an overview of the academic research supporting the effectiveness of questioning, we point you to the excellent book *Quality Questioning* (2017) by Jackie Walsh and Beth Sattes.

In order to make best use of the strategies we offer, consider the following two simple but powerful foundational principles:

1. **Have a Purpose**: Just as with any classroom activity, the questions we ask and the strategies we utilize should have a clear purpose that is aligned to the outcomes we expect from students. Merely posing questions does not guarantee student engagement or learning. The questions we ask and the strategies we utilize should be purposeful and that purpose should be clearly communicated to students. In addition, not all strategies support the same purpose. Some strategies like *I Wonder* focus on getting students to develop their own questions about a topic. Other strategies like *Here's the Question, Find the Answer* and *Who Am I?* require students to interact with their peers in order to grapple with questions. The main point is this: we do not ask questions to simply ask them. We ask questions with a specific purpose and, once that purpose is established, we then look for the most appropriate strategy to meet that purpose.

2. **Pre-Plan Questions**: Grant Wiggins and Jay McTighe, in their highly influential book entitled *Understanding by Design*, probe issues surrounding the importance of planning essential questions and designing lessons so that students come to an understanding of "big" ideas. When planning lessons, they challenge teachers to consider and elaborate on the specific ideas or topics that they want students to understand. This requires that educators carefully pre-plan the questions and questioning strategies and tasks they plan to use in the classroom. Some institutions train teachers to think in terms of Terminal Learning Objectives (TLO). While the use of *terminal* seems a bit gloomy in relation to classroom learning, the point of a TLO is to get educators to consider and describe, in very specific terms, how the learner will be different at the end, or termination, of the lesson. Once the purpose of a lesson has been established,

it is critical to then pre-plan both the specific questions you plan to ask in addition to the specific strategies you plan to use.

Allow us to steal a strategy from the "Writing" section to make our point about the critical importance of purpose and planning *prior* to implementing any of the strategies. If we were to create a *One Word Summary* about purpose and planning, we would use the term *alignment*. Just as an architect needs to align all aspects of a building's design prior to the start of construction, educators must make sure that a clear alignment is in place. Without it, we run the risk of using the wrong designs, the wrong tools, or the wrong strategies. Quite simply, without a clear alignment, we run the risk of increasing boredom rather than battling it.

The academic and intellectual tone of the classroom is largely determined by the quality of the questions being asked by the teacher. Not only do the types of questions matter, but teachers should employ a variety of strategies, techniques, and methods when asking students to answer those questions. In essence, it is imperative to have a deep and varied "toolbox" of questioning strategies in order to engage students.

One final note about questioning. Our bias and belief is that questions serve as a critical foundation for supporting almost everything else that takes place in the classroom. The writing tasks, academic talk, vocabulary development, feedback, and even the use of technology tools require good questions and effective questioning practices.

■ Overview

A focal point is the *thing* that students concentrate their attention on during an academic task. That thing can be an image, a portion of a text, a poster, or a physical location in the classroom. Prompting students where to focus their visual attention helps them to tune out distractions and enhances the quality of their answers.

■ Step by Step

1. Prior to the lesson, prepare some questions and consider the most appropriate visual supports for those questions. In other words, think about what students will be asked to look at while they answer the questions.

2. Get students' attention and prompt them where to look before asking the question. For example, say something like, "Students, I have a couple of questions I want to ask you about the equations we've been factoring. As I ask you these questions, I want you to look at the images I have up here on the screen. You'll need to look up here in order to answer the questions."

3. Pose the question(s) and direct student attention to the *Focal Point*.

■ Tips and Variations

♦ Although this strategy is deceptively simple, it is tremendously powerful because it directs student attention to something specific. Rather than just telling students to "pay attention," this approach tells them to *what to pay attention*.

♦ There are many things that can serve as a *Focal Point*: passages in a book, an artifact, a piece of writing such as a summary, note-taking sheets, or even a specific problem on a practice sheet.

♦ Another reason that external points of reference are so effective is because they help to reduce anxieties or social interaction concerns among students. For example, when combined with a partner activity, this strategy helps students to focus on something external, thus helping students to focus less on *who* they are working with and more on *what* task they are accomplishing.

■ Overview

With a tip of the hat to the game of *Jeopardy*, this strategy provides students with answers and challenges them to find, create, or develop the question(s).

■ Step by Step

1. Prior to the lesson, prepare questions and acceptable answers as you would for any typical question and answer session.

2. Get students' attention and tell them that the class will participate in a question and answer session. However, this session has a twist. Say something like, "Students, there is a popular game show on TV called *Jeopardy*. On the game show, contestants are given the answers and they have to come up with the questions. So, for the next few minutes, I will be giving you some answers and you are going to guess the questions."

3. Model for students what they should say when providing the question. For example, they should say, "What is …?", "Who is …?", "Who are …?", "Where is …?", and so on.

4. Provide an example to students. Say, "The topic is _______. The answer is _______. What's the Question?" Example, "The topic is the solar system. The answer is Mercury, Venus, Earth, and Mars." Acceptable answers: "What are the four inner planets?" or "What are the planets closest to the sun?"

5. Provide think time/wait time.

6. Call on students to provide the question.

■ Tips and Variations

♦ As in the example given in Step 4, there may be more than one acceptable question to an answer.

♦ Some teachers elect to use *Here's the Answer, Find the Question* as a review activity in preparation for assessment. While that is a good use of the strategy, it can also be a unique way to gain student interest at the beginning of a lesson or unit. In that case, create questions and answers that are unusual, interesting, or novel.

♦ Consider placing students with partners or in small groups and have them consult and collaborate on the appropriate question(s).

♦ **Critical Thinking Connection**: An excellent way to challenge learners is to require that they create more than one possible question to the answer. Once an answer has been provided, instruct them to come up with three or four possible questions. Once the answer is provided, ask them to go back and critique which question is the best answer. Ask them to provide a rationale for their choice.

■ Overview

Knowing that what students find interesting, intriguing, or worthy of their time is a key factor in engagement, this strategy uses a simple sentence starter to help identify topics, questions, or issues they want to pursue.

■ Step by Step

1. After reading a text, watching a video, or participating in a discussion tell students that it is their turn to ask some questions about the topic.

2. Provide students with examples of sentence starters such as "I wonder …", "I'm curious about …", or "Why does …"

3. Give them some time to think about the content that was presented. If appropriate, have them consult with partners to discuss what they found interesting.

4. Provide students with the sentence starter and, if necessary, model how to use it.

5. Give students time to write their questions using the sentence starter(s) provided.

6. Place students in partners or small groups to share their *I Wonder* questions or statements.

■ Tips and Variations

♦ A great way to supplement and deepen this strategy is to add extended writing opportunities such as *Fast Writing*; *Write, Talk, Revise*; or *Write On*.

♦ A key to success of this strategy is to provide students with an *experience* prior to asking them to consider what they want to know. For example, have them view a video, look at a *Powerful Image*, or participate in a *QR Hunt*. The point is that students are more likely to consider questions after they have experienced something interesting.

♦ **Critical Thinking Connection**: As students work to create their *I Wonder* questions and statements, provide individual feedback and direction prompting students to analyze the depth of the questions they've created.

■ Overview

The value and impact of wait time, in terms of student engagement, is well established. Some educators prefer to call it *think time* because the purpose is not simply to wait; the goal is to prompt students to think about something. Knowing that some students need additional guidance during wait time/think time, this strategy is helpful in guiding student thinking.

■ Step by Step

1. When planning a lesson, create questions, discussion prompts, or topics that will lead students to think about essential learning.

2. Tell students that you have a question or topic you'd like them to think about. Tell them that this question will require some quiet time so that everyone will have a chance to consider their ideas.

3. Pose the question or provide the prompt and provide appropriate think time.

4. After a few seconds of silence, begin to narrate or describe specific issues, ideas, or elements of the question that you'd like students to think about. For example, when studying the impact of nutrition on people's behavior, say, "Students, I asked you to think about nutrition and how it influences how people behave. But that was a broad question. Think for a minute about what we eat and how that might impact the ability to pay attention in class (provide think time). Have you ever noticed that sometimes it is difficult to pay attention right after lunch (provide think time)?"

■ Tips and Variations

♦ The narration of the think time encourages a narrowing of student thinking. During traditional wait time/think time, we have no way of knowing exactly what students are thinking about. This strategy increases the likelihood that students think about the focus of the question. In other words, the narration funnels their thinking into a specific direction.

♦ For added impact, consider utilizing a *Powerful Image*, an *Audio/Video Example*, or an *Artifact, Realia,* or *Prop* to help narrow student thinking.

♦ **Technology Connection**: Pair this strategy with *Clickers without Clickers* in order to lead a rich class discussion surrounding student responses.

■ Overview

A closed question is one that has a specific, typically short, answer. An open question is one that is "open" to many possible answers. While a closed question requires little more than rote recall, responding to an open question requires elaboration and explanation. In classroom discussions and activities, teachers should use both open and closed questions in order to guide student thinking.

■ Step by Step

1. As you prepare for a lesson, pre-plan both open and closed questions that focus on the objective(s) of the lesson or unit. Examples of open questions include "What are some ways to …", "How might this have been different if …", and "What strategies could be used for …" Examples of closed questions include: "What is …", "Where did …", and How did _____ happen?"

2. Label or sort the questions into a T-chart to evaluate the number, balance, and quality of open and closed questions. The number of open and closed questions does not need to be equal, but you want to ensure you are asking enough open questions to deepen student thinking.

3. Gain student attention and ask open and closed questions. Typically, but not always, teachers elect to begin with a few closed questions to narrow student thinking and then follow up with open questions.

4. If appropriate, support the use of open questions with academic talk, technology, or writing opportunities.

■ Tips and Variations

♦ Some educators have been led to equate open questions as good and closed questions as bad. This is not the case; both are necessary. Closed questions help the teacher to gauge if students have basic, correct information. Open questions help to assess the depth of knowledge.

♦ **Critical Thinking Connection**: Closed questions are, by nature, lower level questions. They typically require little more than rote recall and may not require a significant amount of thought or reflection to answer. Open questions, on the contrary, should be used to expand student thinking as a way to prove their understanding of the content. Utilize a tool such as Bloom's Taxonomy or Webb's Depth of Knowledge to support the creation of open questions.

■ Overview

The adage says that *A picture is worth a thousand words.* So, this strategy relies on the use of pictures, images, and photographs to prompt students to think about and craft questions about a topic.

■ Step by Step

1. Prior to the lesson, collect several images and photos that relate to the objective(s) of the lesson. The images should relate to the objective but be novel, interesting, unexpected, or unusual.

2. Tell students that you'll be showing them some images and pictures and that their job is to look closely at the picture to develop some questions and comments about what they see.

3. Remind students of the objective of the lesson or unit.

4. Show the image(s) and provide students with time to study the image in order to develop thoughts and responses.

5. Prompt students with questions or point out specific parts of the image. For example, when studying concepts related to geometry, show an image of a baseball field and say something like, "Students, we have been discussing angles and shapes in our geometry unit. I want you to take a look at this image of a baseball field in order to see any connections to what we have been studying."

6. If appropriate or necessary, use *Narrated Think Time* to help students notice specific elements of the image.

7. Lead a whole group discussion about what students see in the image(s) and ask them to describe their reactions.

8. Relate the image back to the objective(s) of the lesson.

■ Tips and Variations

♦ A *Powerful Image* is one that evokes some sort of emotional response. The emotional response does not have to be extreme to be effective. A photo that is slightly confusing, humorous, or seemingly contradictory are great examples. In other words, when the students look at the images, you want their curiosity piqued so that they'll begin to ask questions about the topic.

♦ A good way to find *Powerful Images* is to conduct an internet *images* search using key words or topics from the unit of study. In the example above, search for "geometry in real life." Ensure that the images you use from the internet have the appropriate usage rights.

♦ Like the *Questions Only* strategy, this approach is powerful because it requires that students develop, share, and explore *their own* questions about a topic.

Overview

As the name implies, this strategy challenges students to have a discussion where they only exchange questions about a given topic.

Step by Step

1. Place students into pairs or trios.

2. Remind students of the objective(s) of the lesson or unit.

3. If necessary, allow students some time to think about their knowledge of the topic and review materials, resources, or notes.

4. Explain to students that they'll be given a few minutes to have a unique kind of conversation. This conversation requires that partners only ask questions about the topic; they do not provide any answers.

5. Model the process for students using a safe and easy-to-explore topic. For example, you might ask three students to come to the front of the class to have a discussion on the topic of transportation. In this case, the first student might ask something like, "How fast can a jet fly?" Instead of answering that question, the next student offers another closely related question such as, "How high can jets fly?" The students continue to exchange questions until prompted to stop.

6. Explain to students that the *Questions Only* discussion will feel strange at first but that's OK and that it will not feel like a normal conversation.

7. Provide students with a topic or a prompt and instruct them to begin their conversations.

8. If appropriate, lead a whole group discussion on the topic or ask students to do a writing activity to summarize their thinking.

Tips and Variations

♦ This strategy is powerful because it assumes that the questions students generate about a topic or concept is more important than the questions that teachers generate. Students are more likely to engage and explore a topic when they have identified what they want to know about a topic.

♦ The primary challenge of this strategy is that it goes against our natural instinct to answer questions when they are asked of us. Explain to students that it will be difficult not to answer a question, especially when they know the answer.

♦ Do not ask students to have a *Questions Only* discussion on a topic on which they have little or no background. In this case, they don't know what they don't know; so, the strategy will likely stall before it starts.

■ Overview

Too often, educators are fully satisfied when students provide correct answers to questions. However, it is not until we dig deeper that we can discover how well students truly understand something. As a result, this strategy requires students to provide evidence for their answers, beliefs, or statements.

■ Step by Step

1. In preparation for a lesson, pre-plan questions and prompts. Include a variety of both open and closed questions.

2. As you engage students in a question and answer session, follow up their responses with additional questions or statements such as, "Says who?", "Why do you think that?", or "Tell me about your conclusion." The follow-up questions and prompts are aimed at getting students to elaborate, explain, justify their answers, or provide citations.

3. Prior to asking *Says Who?* questions, tell students that there will be times when you do not give them immediate feedback about the accuracy of their answers. Rather, there will be times when you follow up with additional questions that require them to show proof, provide evidence, or give a deeper explanation.

4. Model for students what a *Says Who?* follow-up conversation might sound like. For example, you might say, "Students, there will be occasions when I do not immediately tell you if your answer is right or wrong. Instead, I'll ask follow-up questions so that I can see how deeply you know something. Here is an example, suppose I ask you to estimate the sum of 63 and 98. You guess 150. Now, that might be a right answer, but I may not immediately tell you 'Good job' or 'Yes, you are correct.' Instead, I'll ask you to elaborate and explain. In other words, I'll expect you to explain your answer. By the way, just because I provide a follow-up question does not mean you are wrong, so there is no need to be insecure about your answers. Rather, I am just digging deeper to see how well you know something."

■ Tips and Variations

♦ It is important to note that *Says Who?* or any follow-up question(s) should not be said with a hint of disbelief, distrust, or sarcasm. And, it should never be used in an attempt to embarrass a student or publicly point out their misunderstanding of something.

♦ In an attempt to get the strategy on one page, delete all these lines. Keep the Critical Thinking Connection.

♦ **Critical Thinking Connection**: Utilize academic talk or writing-to-learn strategies to require students to analyze the depth of their answers and ideas. Teach students to ask follow-up questions of themselves and their peers with questions like, "On a scale of one to ten, how confident are you of that answer?" or "If you had to talk about this idea for 2 minutes, what would you say?"

■ Overview

Similar to other question stems such as *I Wonder*, this strategy prompts students to think about alternative answers, different ideas, or diverse perspectives. Simply put, it requires that students dig deeper into their thinking in order to imagine different responses or scenarios.

■ Step by Step

1. As you prepare for the lesson, pre-plan open-ended questions or prompts that require students to wonder about different outcomes. For example, when learning about the role of the allied powers in World War II, ask students to think about the outcome of the war had the United States not become involved. Or, ask students to consider the outcome had the United States become involved sooner.

2. At appropriate times during the lesson, stop and ask students to imagine different scenarios, outcomes, or *What Ifs*.

3. Provide students with appropriate wait time and, if necessary, provide *Narrated Think Time*.

4. Ask students to share their ideas with a partner or lead them in a writing-to-learn strategy such as *Fast Writing*.

5. Lead a whole group discussion elaborating on student ideas and providing feedback about the accuracy of their ideas.

■ Tips and Variations

♦ As is the case with many of the strategies in this book, students will benefit from starting off with a simple model where you ask them *What If ...* questions about something they have high levels of interest or background in. For example, you could ask them, "What would happen if the internet was not available for an entire week?"

♦ **Critical Thinking Connection**: Encourage students to dig into the content to create their own *What If ...* questions.

♦ **Technology Connection**: Pair this strategy with *Collaborative Sticky Notes* or *Backchannels* and allow students to post their questions and seek answers from each other.

Who Am I?

■ Overview

This strategy utilizes the classic game format of 20 Questions to get students to think about important questions. While the name implies the answers should be a *person*, the strategy is flexible and can include alternatives such as *What Am I?* and *Where Am I?*

■ Step by Step

1. Prior to the lesson, assemble a list of people, terminology, facts, or locations that are essential to the learning objective(s).

2. Create slips of paper containing the information you've created in Step 1. Place those slips of paper into an envelope. Create enough slips and envelopes for several small groups.

3. Remind students of the objective(s) of the lesson and tell them that they'll have an opportunity to play a game similar to 20 Questions.

4. Place students into groups of three to five and provide each group with an envelope.

5. Model for students the process of playing the game of *Who Am I?* The first student reaches into the envelope and pulls out a slip of paper. Without showing their partners what is written on the paper, they read to themselves the fact, name, or term on the slip. When ready, they entertain questions from the other members of the group. Members of the group ask questions such as, "Is it a person?", "Have we spoken about this in the last week?", or "Is this related to …" All of the questions need to be answered with only a *yes* or a *no*. Members of the group continue to ask questions until someone is ready to guess what is written on the slip of paper.

6. When a student guesses the answer correctly, it is then their turn to pull a slip of paper from the envelope.

7. Continue the process until all the slips of paper have been discussed.

■ Tips and Variations

♦ This is an excellent strategy to support vocabulary development. Consider combining it with *Act It Out* or use the same words utilized in *Concentration Plus*.

♦ **Differentiation Connection:** Depending on the needs of the students, you could allow them to ask more or less than 20 questions. In addition, it may be wise to allow the first partner to give some clues or hints.

Part Five

Technology

Key Idea: *Today's students seem to be naturally engaged by technology. It draws them in and they tend to have a better understanding of the technology than many teachers. Although it can be scary as a teacher to incorporate technology into the classroom, it is an excellent way to get students engaged in important learning tasks.*

Technology—just the word seems to evoke emotion from students and teachers, whether it be excitement or fear. No matter the emotion it evokes from us as educators, we need to understand that it is a different world for our students. Google incorporated in 1998, Facebook launched in 2004, YouTube started in 2005, the Apple iPhone was released in 2007, and the Apple iPad was released in 2010. The world in which our students are growing up is different: touch screens are the norm, "Google it" and "YouTube it" are common phrases, and the science fiction technology of past generations is now a reality.

So, let's embrace this reality. The thoughtful and effective use of technology can lead to increased engagement and learning for our students. Quite simply, integrating technology tools into your classroom repertoire is an excellent way to battle boredom. Classroom teacher and 2011 ASCD Young Educator Award Winner, Brad Kuntz (2012), said it well:

> Technology is not our enemy. With some patience, careful planning, and thoughtful consideration, we will create more skilled students who are ready for the future, while creating a more enriching classroom dynamic where technology is just another tool for building students' success.

Let's utilize the passion our students have for technology and show them how it can be used to both enhance their learning and prepare them for the future. Their future isn't going to be less filled with technology; students will be exposed to more and more technology in an ever-changing world. Those teachers who refuse to use technology are missing out on an extremely valuable tool to engage students in learning.

Consider the story of Jesus, one of Lisa's eighth grade students when she was a middle school technology teacher. By almost every measure, he was an unsuccessful student: he was failing all his classes, he hated to write, and he struggled in most academic classes. When he was asked to write a traditional, pencil-and-paper personal narrative, he struggled to get his thoughts and ideas on paper. However, when he was given the opportunity to use technology to tell his story, he produced some of the most well-thought-out and emotional videos Lisa had ever seen. To tell his story, Jesus had to write a script, create a storyboard, gather images, find appropriate music that was legal to use, create transitions and effects, and narrate the story. He put a tremendous amount of effort into the task and he persisted far beyond the required elements of the assignment.

Jesus's story illustrates the power of technology to engage students in meaningful learning. To students (and to many adults as well) technology offers freedom, flexibility, and a level of creativity not offered in traditional classroom assignments. A number of academic research studies support this idea as well. Linda Darling-Hammond and her colleagues (2014) summarized it well when they said:

> [S]tudies have found that students demonstrate stronger engagement, self-efficacy, attitudes toward school, and skill development when they are engaged in content

creation projects. Among other examples, this can include engaging in multimedia content creation to communicate ideas about the material they are studying by creating reports, graphic representations of data they have researched or developed, websites, PowerPoint presentations, video production, digital storytelling, and other means.

As you work to integrate technology into your lessons, consider some additional thoughts about the relationship between engagement, learning, and technology in the classroom:

♦ Up to 93 percent of teachers use technology to guide instruction (Bill and Melinda Gates Foundation, 2015). From accessing an online curriculum to utilizing technology-based assessments, technology tools and resources play a significant role in our profession. Since technology tools are seeing an increased use in classrooms, Lee Brenner (2015) points out that "It's critical that teachers understand how to effectively use technology to enhance their lessons and increase their students' retention, comprehension and engagement."

♦ Keeping students engaged while integrating technology requires a shift from "passive" to "active" uses of the technology (Herold, 2016). Students should not be passively watching their teachers use technology; rather, students should actively use the technology to learn, research, and create.

♦ We must be careful not to assume that our students know how to use all of the technology at their disposal. Their level of digital literacy may not be where we think it is; while students may know how to use a certain piece of technology outside of school, they may lack the skills and knowledge in how to use it for an academic task. Training students in the appropriate academic use of technology is a necessity.

♦ While technology is a powerful engagement tool, it is important to utilize it in authentic ways. Be cautious not to just incorporate technology for technology's sake. It should be integrated in a meaningful way that is part of an overall plan. Digital literacy leader and author Eric Sheninger (2015) cautions:

> If the emphasis is on digital learning we must not get caught up in the bells and whistles or smoke and mirrors that are commonly associated with the digital aspect alone. Engagement should always translate into deeper learning opportunities where technology provides students the means to think critically and solve problems while demonstrating what they know and can do in a variety of ways.

When considering the strategies we describe in this section, remember that student engagement is the target. The use of technology tools and resources may not make the job of teaching any easier. In other words, these are not "Sit at your desk and get caught up on grading" types of tasks. In all honesty, the more we work with teachers who are integrating technology into their classrooms, the more we are aware that the technology does not necessarily make classroom life any easier. In fact, in the beginning stages, there is a bit of a learning curve and time needs to be devoted to planning and organization. However, teachers consistently report that the efforts are worth the investment. Just as Jesus experienced a renewed sense of engagement and learning because he was offered the chance to use technology, your students will also benefit from your time and investment.

■ Overview

This strategy calls for students to use an online program or an app to annotate images and photographs. These annotations can be completed individually, with partners, as a small group, or even as a note-taking strategy.

■ Step by Step

1. Take a picture or locate an image of an item or concept you wish to annotate.

2. On a computer or tablet, open the image using an editing program such as Pic Monkey—www.picmonkey.com. (Additional editing tools are listed below under "Technology Resources.")

3. Add annotations such as comments, highlights, arrows, titles and icons to elaborate and add meaning to the image.

■ Tips and Variations

♦ This strategy allows for a lot of creativity on the part of students. Remind them that images do not always have to be of concrete items; they could annotate images of solved math problems or abstract concepts such as resilience and perseverance.

♦ Many teachers combine this strategy with a *Camera Scavenger Hunt* by having students annotate pictures they have taken.

♦ When using online images, be conscious of copyright laws. This is an opportunity to teach students about how to legally use online images.

♦ **Differentiation Connection:** *Annotated Images* can be an alternative method for note taking for those students who struggle taking traditional notes. Provide these students with an image on which to annotate or provide a cloze note version of annotations on an image for those who need extra support.

♦ **Technology Resources:**

Fotor—www.fotor.com

Pic Collage——www.pic-collage.com

Skitch——www.evernote.com/skitch

Explain Everything——www.explaineverything.com

Pixlr——www.pixlr.com

■ Overview

During class, whether it be during a traditional mini-lecture, group work, or independent work time, this strategy provides students an opportunity to post questions and comments related to the content in an online conversation tool called a backchannel.

■ Step by Step

1. Set up a backchannel portal using an online resource such as www.edmodo.com.
2. Give students the information about how to access the backchannel, including the web address, sign up codes, or passwords.
3. Model for students how to post questions and comments in the backchannel portal.
4. At various points during the lesson or unit, prompt students to post comments and questions to the teacher and to each other.

■ Tips and Variations

- It's a good idea to introduce the backchannel tool prior to having students use it for an academic purpose. Provide students with time to log in, become acquainted with the format and icons, and "play" with the site. Once they are familiar with how to use the tool, slowly increase the duration and complexity of the activities students are to utilize.

- Make the expectations for use of the backchannel very clear to students—it is for academic purposes only. Tell students that comments such as "What's up?" or other unrelated posts will be deleted.

- The backchannel can also serve as an excellent informal assessment tool. The questions that students ask and the responses that they give will provide valuable information for re-teaching and enrichment opportunities.

- **Differentiation Connection**: Depending on the maturity level and needs of your students, provide models and examples of appropriate posts, questions, and comments. As students become more comfortable (and responsible) with the use of the backchannel, allow them to answer each other's questions and comment on each other's posts.

- **Technology Resources**:

    Todays Meet—www.todaysmeet.com

    Backchannel Chat—www.backchannelchat.com

    Padlet—www.padlet.com

    Lino—www.linoit.com

Camera Scavenger Hunt

■ Overview

This strategy requires students to go on a scavenger hunt using a camera to find examples of a specific concept.

■ Step by Step

1. Remind students of the objective(s) and focus of the lesson or unit.

2. Tell students that they will be given some time to do a very special kind of scavenger hunt; one that involves the use of a camera (or a device with a camera such as an iPad or cell phone) to find examples of concepts and ideas from the unit of study. For students that may be unfamiliar with the concept of a scavenger hunt, provide them with details, examples, and explanations.

3. Give students the topic or a list of items they will be looking for during their scavenger hunt. For example, when studying angles, tell students that they'll be looking around the classroom for examples of obtuse, acute, and right angles.

4. Show some examples and then provide students with time to wander the classroom with a camera or a device to find and capture the examples.

5. Once students have found examples, ask them to share their work with classmates, have them post the images to a class website, or have students use the images in a presentation they create.

6. Use the examples students have gathered as an informal assessment tool to gauge the depth of student knowledge and understanding.

■ Tips and Variations

♦ Depending on the objective(s) and ability level of the students, encourage them to look outside the classroom for examples of the concept or idea being studied.

♦ This strategy is extremely flexible—it can be as simple as asking students to find examples of the primary colors to as advanced as having students document examples of abstract concepts like cooperation.

♦ If students have devices they take home, the scavenger hunt could be expanded to their neighborhoods and other places the students may go such as the grocery store or baseball field. In this way, it can serve as a novel and unique homework assignment.

♦ The scavenger hunt could be combined with *Annotated Images*. After completing the scavenger hunt, students could annotate the images to explain the examples they found.

♦ **Differentiation Connection**: This strategy is a great way to incorporate movement in the classroom, as students will be encouraged to move about to find examples. This strategy could also be offered as an alternative choice to traditional assignments for those students who need extra opportunities for purposeful movement.

■ Overview

This strategy combines two approaches that are deeply motivating for students: using technology and the ability to make choices during their learning. A technology-based choice board is easily differentiated and allows teachers to quickly assess student progress.

■ Step by Step

1. Create a 3-row by 3-column chart using Microsoft Word, Excel, or an online tool such as Blendspace—www.tes.com/lessons.

2. In each box, include a different technology-based activity that aligns with the lesson or unit objective(s). Activities could include a link to a video or a website, a QR code that links to an article that students must read, an online simulation or a game, or a *Backchannel* conversation tool such as Edmodo.

3. Introduce the concept of a choice board by instructing students that they will have some options with the activities they complete. Provide students with examples and model the use of the choice board including what to do if a particular technology-based activity does not work properly.

4. Tell students that they will be responsible for something like a game of Tic-Tac-Toe. That is, they must complete three activities in a row. They get to make the selections and determine in which order they complete the tasks.

5. Provide each student with a handout of the choice board chart and give them directions for how much time they have to complete their row of activities.

■ Tips and Variations

♦ Give some thought and planning to the types of activities that will be included in each row and column, making sure that essential learning activities are spaced appropriately. In addition, if there is an activity that you want all students to complete, it can be included more than once on the choice board.

♦ Additional ideas for choices include creation of an infographic, a journal entry, an *Annotated Image*, a poster, or use of a *Digital Whiteboard*.

♦ As students become proficient and responsible with their choice boards, consider expanding the grids to 4 × 4 or 5 × 5.

♦ **Critical Thinking Connection:** Use a resource such as Bloom's Taxonomy or Webb's Depth of Knowledge to expand the types of activities and outcomes included on the choice board.

♦ **Technology Resources:** Additional ideas can be found at the following websites:

    Padlet—www.padlet.com

    Lino—www.linoit.com

    Thinglink—https://www.thinglink.com

■ Overview

Technology-based student response systems are handheld devices (and the accompanying software) commonly referred to as "clickers." While early versions of the systems were somewhat complicated, they offered teachers a chance to pose a question or a prompt and get immediate feedback from every student. With the evolution of the devices and software, student response systems have become much more user friendly for teachers and students. The most current versions allow students to use their own devices as "clickers."

■ Step by Step

1. Prior to using a student response system, create questions, prompts, or quiz questions that relate to the objective of the lesson.

2. Select a software tool, such as Socrative, Kahoot, or Plickers, and acquaint yourself with the format and options within the program.

3. Utilize the chosen tool to enter questions, prompts, answer choices, or survey questions and set any necessary preferences.

4. Introduce students to the tool and allow them some time to "play" within the system to become acquainted with how it works.

5. When you are ready to use the system, provide students with directions and information about how to access the activities. Ensure that you schedule enough time for any troubleshooting that may need to take place.

6. Using the system, pose questions or prompts and require that students use their device(s) to respond.

■ Tips and Variations

♦ Since most student response systems provide immediate feedback, the data collected provides an excellent source of information that can be used to make instructional decisions for the current and future lessons.

♦ Do not introduce too many different student response systems to students in a short amount of time. Use each tool several times prior to introducing a new one, as each tool has unique features.

♦ **Technology Resources**: Each of the response systems listed below offers something unique that the others do not. Spend some time researching which option is best for your students. While this is not an exhaustive list, it does include the more commonly used tools:

Socrative—www.socrative.com

Kahoot—www.getkahoot.com

Go Formative—www.goformative.com

Plickers—www.plickers.com

■ Overview

This strategy allows students to post virtual "sticky notes" onto a collaborative web page to cooperate, share ideas, organize their thinking, and receive feedback on their progress. Students can also post text, images, website links, and videos (depending on the tool being used).

■ Step by Step

1. Spend some time researching the tool (app or website) that will best meet the needs of your students. Popular tools include www.padlet.com, www.note.ly, www.linoit.com, and www.scrumblr.ca.

2. Prior to presenting the tool to your students, gather some examples and ideas of the types of things students can and should post to the website. Examples might include summaries, questions, responses to other students' ideas, or facts learned.

3. Spend some time within the program ensuring that network and sharing permissions are set appropriately. This would include password information and whether the information will be public or hidden.

4. Give students information about how to access the website.

5. Show students examples of what kinds of information and topic(s) should be included on the collaborative sticky notes.

6. Prompt students with a question or a task and allow them time to create and post their sticky notes.

7. Give students time to browse the site to create, view, and/or respond to other students' sticky notes.

■ Tips and Variations

♦ An excellent way to save time is to create a QR code with the website link so students can simply scan the code and go directly to the site instead of spending time entering a lengthy or complicated web address.

♦ Ensure that all permissions are set properly. Some sites default to a view only or private mode, which would make it difficult for students to collaborate.

♦ **Differentiation Connection**: Allow students to work with partners or small groups to tackle a task such as a research project. As the teacher, these tools make it easy to view the efforts and participation of all students. In addition, the nature of the tool makes accessing information and notes simple for students who tend to be disorganized.

Collage

■ Overview

Think back to the days of creating a traditional collage—glue, scissors, old magazines, and carefully planning where everything should go. Once something was glued, it was difficult to edit, change, or correct. However, technology now allows students to create a collage that is easy to use, interactive, and fun to create.

■ Step by Step

1. Select a program such as Microsoft PowerPoint, Word, or an online website such as www.pic-collage.com. Spend some time acquainting yourself with the features of the program, including backgrounds available, images, fonts, and templates.

2. Introduce the concept of a collage to your students and show some examples and models.

3. Lead students to open a blank document, slideshow, or the collage app or website.

4. Prompt students to draw pictures, insert images, and add words to design a collage that illustrates a concept or idea.

5. As students are working on their collages, provide feedback, answer questions, and prompt students to consider different design elements.

■ Tips and Variations

♦ Consider combining this strategy with a *Camera Scavenger Hunt* to allow students to include images and photographs that they have taken themselves.

♦ Many teachers opt to use a technology-based collage to help students build vocabulary knowledge. In this way, it can become a technological version of *Illustrated Vocabulary*.

♦ **Critical Thinking Connection**: Once students have completed their collage, lead them through a process of analyzing their own work. Ask them questions such as, "Are there any images you didn't include that would have helped the overall project?", or "How could you use this collage to explain this concept to a younger student?"

■ Overview

As an engagement strategy, *Digital Whiteboards* offer students a chance to manipulate information using a flexible, interactive software tool that allows them to draw, use color, save, and review what they've created on their whiteboard. Used in place of a regular whiteboard, it can greatly increase engagement and allows students to save their work to review at a later time or to turn in to the teacher.

■ Step by Step

1. Instruct students to open the whiteboard app or website, such as the Notes App on an iPad, or the website Scribblar.com.

2. Students use the whiteboard app as they would use a traditional whiteboard to complete tasks such as writing words, solving problems, or illustrating a concept. For example, when working with a small group, you may choose to have students write words from a book that follow a certain vowel pattern and underline the vowel pattern in a different color. Another example would be for students to solve a math problem, writing the original problem in one color and solving the problem in another color.

3. Students can then save the whiteboard as a picture file or whiteboard file (depending on the software or app). If the program doesn't allow you to save as a picture, take a screenshot instead.

4. Student work can be used in an assignment or project, to review at a later time, or to turn in for an informal assessment. If it is not necessary to save, students can simply erase the board or start a new file without saving the changes.

■ Tips and Variations

- Utilize color to your advantage—use different colors for different sounds in a word (for example, a "ck" digraph is always blue; onsets in red and rhymes in black; or ones, tens, and hundreds in three different colors).

- Consider pairing this strategy with *Annotated Images*. In this case, have students insert a picture on to the digital whiteboard in order to annotate it.

- Use collaborative features of online whiteboards so multiple students can work on the same board. You may choose to have each student use a different color so you can see what each student contributed to the board.

- **Technology Resources**
    - Notes App (iPad)
    - Kids Doodle (iPad)
    - Paper by 53—www.fiftythree.com
    - Scoot & Doodle and ScoodleJam—www.scootdoodle.com
    - Twiddla—www.twiddla.com
    - Scribblar—scribblar.com

■ Overview

Using a device that has the ability to record audio or video, students record themselves as they describe, explain, and elaborate on their knowledge of a subject.

■ Step by Step

1. Spend some time becoming acquainted with web tools and apps that can be used to save and play back audio and video recordings. Popular options include www.showme.com, www.explaineverything.com, www.educreations.com, and www.doceri.com.

2. Introduce students to the app or web tool and tell them that they'll be recording summaries, conversations, and discussions centered on the concept(s) you've been studying.

3. Provide students with some models and examples of how to *Explain Your Thinking* and allow them some time to become acquainted with the tools and features of the website or app.

4. Lead students to write a script that will explain the concept being studied. If appropriate and allowable with the selected technology, allow students to insert images that will help to explain the concept.

5. Prompt students to record themselves explaining the concept and any images that were included.

6. Once the recordings are completed, students play back their audio or video to analyze their work. If needed, students can re-record and correct or add information.

■ Tips and Variations

♦ When students explain their thinking via an audio or video recording, it provides an excellent source of information for assessment purposes.

♦ Consider combining *Explain Your Thinking* with *Conferencing* to allow the student one-on-one time with the teacher.

♦ Student recordings can be shared with parents to illustrate successes or struggles in the classroom, opening the door to further conversations with the families.

■ Overview

This strategy combines novelty, movement, and traditional academic strategies into an activity that requires students to use technology to navigate and interact with content.

■ Step by Step

1. Prior to introducing students to the *QR Hunt*, create a list of questions and activities related to the objective(s) of the lesson or unit.

2. Using a QR code maker such as www.qrcode-monkey.com or www.qrafter.com, create questions, prompts, or activities and link each one to a different QR code. During the process of creating the codes, make sure to document which codes align with which activities.

3. Print posters or documents with the QR codes and place them at various locations around the classroom.

4. Provide students with a handout or a graphic organizer to utilize while hunting for the QR codes.

5. Provide students with a device such as a tablet or an iPod that will read QR codes and prompt them to locate the codes placed around the room.

■ Tips and Variations

♦ As with many of the technology-based strategies shared throughout this chapter, it is important to model for students exactly what is expected of them as they use the technology. In addition, tell students what to do in case the technology does not work as expected.

♦ QR codes are simply links to websites that, once the code is scanned, will take the device to the desired website. As such, they are very versatile. Many teachers use the codes to link to videos, images, or documents that reinforce the concept being studied. In fact, textbook publishers often insert QR codes into their instructional resources.

♦ **Differentiation Connection**: QR codes are easy to differentiate. Simply provide students with different QR codes, depending on their needs and ability level, in order to complete different activities or answer different questions.

Vocabulary

Key Idea: *Mastering, understanding, and using essential academic vocabulary is a hallmark of being educated in every academic discipline. A deep, rich, and properly used vocabulary sets students up for success in school and in life. However, not all instructional strategies are equally effective at engaging students in the development and use of vocabulary.*

There is an ancient proverb, most often contributed to Confucius, that says, *I hear and I forget. I see and I remember. I do and I understand.* When it comes to learning, remembering, and understanding important academic vocabulary, this proverb fits perfectly. Too often educators rely on vocabulary development strategies that simply do not work; we give students words to look up in a dictionary, to copy, and to use in artificial sentences, or we rely on tests and quizzes to ensure that students learn the vocabulary. However, when it comes to true understanding, students need to be actively engaged *with* the vocabulary. A deep, rich, and accurate academic vocabulary requires students to be actively and authentically engaged. In other words, they need to *do*. Vocabulary is not something we do to students, it is something they develop through multiple, meaningful, and engaging exposures where students have to use the vocabulary in authentic ways.

Why is vocabulary development important? Quite simply, vocabulary development impacts everything—comprehension, grades, intelligence, and even an individual's income potential later in life (Marzano, Pickering, and Pollack, 2001). While a comprehensive overview of vocabulary instruction is beyond the scope of this chapter, here we offer a few words of wisdom from some educators and researchers who have thought deeply about this subject:

- According to Eric Jensen, author of *Engaging Students with Poverty in Mind* (2013), vocabulary development is a key factor in increasing achievement and engagement among students of poverty. He reminds teachers that we must be "relentless" in helping students build vocabulary knowledge and understanding.

- In perhaps the most seminal study of vocabulary development outside of school, Hart and Risely (1995) found that there was as much as a 30-million-word gap in the number of words spoken in the homes of poor families when compared with professional families. This study focused on the number of words young children heard from birth to age 4. This means that children of poverty enter school with a significant gap in vocabulary development.

- Marzano, Pickering, and Pollack, in their popular and influential book *Classroom Instruction that Works* (2001), emphasize that students need to encounter words in multiple contexts on multiple occasions in order to learn them. Furthermore, the National Institute of Child Health and Human Development (2000) underscore the necessity for teachers to provide multiple instructional methods to teach vocabulary. In other words, a single exposure to a word using one instructional strategy will not result in optimal learning for students.

- One study found that young children who played with good old-fashioned wooden blocks during learning time developed increased vocabulary (Ferrara et al., 2011). Play time, it seems, is critical to developing and using vocabulary.

- Paula Rutherford, in her book *Why Didn't I Learn This in College* (2009), reminds teachers that instructional strategies that build vocabulary must include three essential elements: mastery, retention, and transfer. In other words, students need to use the vocabulary correctly, remember it over time, and transfer the use of the vocabulary to different contexts inside and outside of school.

- As educators, we owe a tremendous debt of gratitude to researchers such as Stephen Krashen, Jim Cummins, Deborah Short, and Jana Echevarria, who have spent decades studying second language acquisition. They remind us that language (including vocabulary) is acquired through a natural process that involves an individual's genuine interaction with words and concepts. Too often vocabulary learning in school is artificial and forced rather than natural and genuine.

- In one of the more seminal studies on vocabulary development, Margaret McKeown and colleagues (1985) found that students needed a minimum of 12 interactions with a new word before comprehension improved.

- Students should be taught technical and specialized academic vocabulary in advance of lessons and be required to use that vocabulary in their collaborative and independent tasks (Fisher, Frey, and Pumpian, 2012).

- Literacy guru Timothy Rasinski and colleagues (2012) outline several misconceptions about vocabulary development. Among them is the assumption that dictionary definitions are sufficient in helping students develop vocabulary. In reality, dictionary definitions fall short in helping students to truly understand a word. For a student to really understand a word, they need to also know structure, pronunciation, grammar, semantics, and spelling. Rasinski advocates for ditching the weekly vocabulary lists which he describes them as "drudgery" and highlights the fact that they do not lead to long-term learning.

For those who want to dig into the research a bit more, we'd point you to the following excellent resources: *Bringing Words to Life* (2013), by Isabel Beck and colleagues, and *Vocabulary Instruction: Research to Practice* (2012), edited by James Bauman and Edward Kame'enui. Additionally, there are some well-researched and strategy-rich articles and web resources that provide great insights for classroom teachers. A couple of our favorites are *Nine Things Every Teacher Should Know about Words and Vocabulary Instruction* (2007), by Karen Bromley, and *Vocabulary: Five Common Misconceptions*, by Nancy Padak and colleagues (2012).

The strategies we offer here focus on helping students develop vocabulary for academic disciplines; that is, they help students to master those technical words, phrases, and terms that are essential for success in the classroom. While *Battling Boredom Part 2* is a book of strategies, effective vocabulary development is about explicit, focused instruction. It is not enough to simply assign vocabulary tasks to students; we do not want to reinforce the idea that strategies alone are sufficient. Strategies are part of a thoughtful, planned, and systematic approach to teaching vocabulary.

One final note about the importance of vocabulary development. Perhaps more than any other category or topic we discuss in this book, vocabulary is linked to everything else. For students to have quality academic discussions, they need to utilize accurate vocabulary. Likewise, the strategies offered in the writing, feedback, questioning, and technology sections all rely on students understanding and accurately using vocabulary.

■ Overview

Just as the name implies, this strategy gets students to act out vocabulary terms, phrases, or concepts.

■ Step by Step

1. Prior to the use of this strategy, create a list of terms, phrases, or words that are essential to the objective(s) of the lesson or unit.

2. Write each of the words on index cards, one word per card. Create several sets of cards for as many groups as necessary.

3. Divide the class into groups of six to eight students per group.

4. Give each group a stack of index cards.

5. If students are unfamiliar with the game of charades, take a few minutes to explain the rules, show some examples, and model the process.

6. Prompt the first student in the group to select a card (without looking). That student reads the card, considers how to get their peers to guess the word, and then creates motions, actions, or movements to convey the word. Each student is given 1 minute to act out the word they've selected. Other students in the group are tasked with guessing the answer.

7. At the end of the minute, if no one has guessed the correct answer, the actor tells the group the word.

8. Continue the process until all students have a chance to act out a word or until all cards are utilized.

9. If appropriate, lead a whole group discussion on the process of acting out their words. Ask questions such as, "Which words seemed most difficult?" or "In what other ways might we have expressed that idea?"

■ Tips and Variations

♦ A great way to reinforce vocabulary from past units or assignments is to mix up new and old words together. In this way, you can "spiral" back to previously used words to reinforce their use.

♦ Many students will benefit from the opportunity to "pass" or select a different card. In those cases, instruct students to set that card aside so it is not selected by another student.

♦ **Differentiation Connection:** Different sets of cards and words can be provided to different groups depending on their needs, language ability, and background knowledge. In addition, it may be appropriate for some students to be given permission to use one or two key words along with their movements.

Banned Words

■ Overview

Quite simply, *Banned Words* are those phrases, terms, words, or vocabulary that are designated for non-use during a specific task or assignment. "Banned" words are not bad words in the traditional sense; rather, students are challenged to give up the use of certain words in order to expand their vocabulary.

■ Step by Step

1. Prior to the lesson or unit, give some consideration to the words or phrases that you find students using too often. For example, during a creative writing assignment, you might find students overusing words like *said*, *also*, and certain pronouns such as *I*.

2. Tell students they are no longer allowed to use these words during their writing or in their speaking. Display the words and lead a brief discussion about why the words are banned. Make sure that you do not ban necessary words like "the" or "and."

3. Explain to students that you understand that it may be difficult to stop using the word, but you are sure that they can grow their vocabulary and gain a richer store of language by using alternatives that may better describe their thoughts and ideas.

4. Depending on the age of your students and the depth of their vocabulary, you may need to provide alternatives to the banned words. If so, have students help brainstorm the alternatives with you.

■ Tips and Variations

♦ Teachers sometimes wonder about exceptions. Are there any times when a student is allowed to use a banned word? Yes, but consult with the students and ask them to provide a rationale for why the chosen word is the best choice and why other words are not sufficient to communicate their idea.

♦ If a student uses a banned word, ask them if they can rephrase what they've said using a different word or phrase. The point is not to punish or scold students for using banned words; the goal is to expand the words and vocabulary they use. For students that struggle to come up with alternative words or phrases, provide some suggestions and feedback via *Conferencing* or *Anchors*.

♦ **Technology Connection**: Allow, and even encourage, the use of a digital thesaurus or a synonym feature in a word processing program. Students need to become as familiar with these tools as they are with a traditional dictionary or thesaurus.

■ Overview

Every academic discipline has its own set of words, phrases, and vocabulary that can be difficult for students to comprehend and use. Knowing that some of those challenging words are also essential for students to know and understand, this strategy pre-teaches students so they know what to do when they encounter those big words.

■ Step by Step

1. Preview the text(s) that students will be reading. During that preview, compile a list of any words, phrases, or terminology that may cause confusion among your students. Note that some big words might be common words that are used in a unique or odd way within the text.

2. When introducing the text to students, point out those words. Say something like, "Students, in just a moment we are going to read a short article on the concept of lift as it relates to how planes can fly. But, before we read that article, I want to give you a heads up—a warning—that some of the words you are going to read can be confusing. I call them big words. So, this is your big word alert. The following terms may be easy to spell and pronounce, but they can be a bit tricky if we don't understand how they are used by this author."

3. Introduce the words to the students and provide brief definitions, background, or images to support their understanding.

4. After a discussion or mini-lecture on the words, introduce the text and ask students to pay special attention when they come across the big words.

■ Tips and Variations

◆ Not all big words are actually "big" words. In other words, some words may not be difficult to pronounce, spell, or define, but they may have multiple meanings or nuances (such as a confusing homonym) that are essential for student understanding.

◆ It is important to note that this strategy needs to be used sparingly. Not all words can be big words. In any given text, there may be many words or phrases that are important, but not all are truly essential to the objective of the lesson.

◆ Allow students the opportunity for academic talk as they encounter the big words. Let them discuss the words and their significance to the text and to the learning objective.

◆ **Differentiation Connection:** Not all students need to be pre-taught the same big words. While a whole class discussion would require the same words for everyone, consider conducting a couple of small group instruction sessions to provide varied levels of support (and words) to different groups of students.

Concentration Plus

Overview

The classic matching game of concentration is a great way to reinforce and develop vocabulary. This strategy adds a twist—a plus—to the game that requires students to use their words once they've collected matching cards.

Step by Step

1. In preparation for the game, create sets of note cards containing words and definitions of terms, concepts, and ideas related to the objective(s) of the lesson or unit. Write the words on one set of cards and their definitions on another set. Ensure that each word card has a matching definition card. Shuffle all the cards together and place them in a pile.

2. Explain the rules of the game of concentration: All cards should be placed face down on a table or on the floor. Students take turns turning cards over looking to match words and their definitions. When a student makes a match, they keep both the word and definition cards. A student who makes a successful match gets another turn. Students continue to take turns until all the card sets have been collected.

3. If necessary, model for students what the game looks like and (depending on the students) how to graciously win or lose the game.

4. Once students finish the game, introduce them to the "plus" part of *Concentration Plus*. This refers to what students are to do with their word and definition cards. Tell students that they will use the cards they've collected to complete one or more of the following tasks: use them as part of a partner discussion, use them to write a summary or a story, create a list of associated words, draw pictures of the words, and so on.

5. Provide time for students to complete their plus activities.

Tips and Variations

♦ *Concentration Plus* is not just for younger students and simple words. The real power of this strategy is the additional tasks students are required to do once they have collected the word cards. The wider variety of ways that students interact with the words, the better. The game of concentration is simply a fun and novel way to get students to collect words that they'll be required to use.

♦ Some teachers elect to use this strategy as a centers-based activity. In this case, make sure that there is accountability for the "plus" activities that students complete.

♦ **Differentiation Connection**: There are a variety of different tasks students can complete during the "plus" phase of this strategy. Some students may simply need to play the game again while other students could use technology to design an *Annotated Image*. In addition, it is prudent to provide different groups of students with different card sets. In this way, all students could be required to complete the same "plus" using different words.

■ Overview

When it comes to vocabulary development, a picture is worth far more than a thousand words. This strategy requires that students provide an illustration of their understanding of an important word or concept.

■ Step by Step

1. Prior to the lesson, make a list of those terms, concepts, or ideas that are most essential to the learning objective.

2. Tell students about the power of images and illustrations when it comes to helping to understand something. Perhaps share examples of richly decorated illustrations from books, magazines, or historical documents.

3. Give students the word or words they will be illustrating.

4. Explain the difference between an illustration and a sketch or doodle. Illustrations have details, they take planning and thought, and they help to convey meaning, while sketches provide very little detail, they are typically done quickly, and they are usually unnecessary for one to truly understand a concept.

5. Provide time for students to think about the word, research its meaning, and talk with their peers about the word.

6. Prompt students to plan and design their illustration, possibly starting with a rough draft.

7. When students are ready, have them begin working on their illustrations.

8. Once the illustration is finished, give students an opportunity to provide an explanation, either in writing or verbally, of how and why they chose to illustrate the vocabulary word in the manner they chose.

■ Tips and Variations

♦ *Illustrated Vocabulary* is much more than a simple sketch, drawing, or doodle. Rather, think of illustrations in terms of the artwork and imagery that an author has included in a book. True illustrations tell part of the story and help to convey meaning.

♦ **Critical Thinking Connection:** Give students two to three words to combine into one illustration. Ask them to include connections, relationships, or distinctions between the words.

♦ **Technology Connection:** Students can use coding or stop-motion software to create animations of the vocabulary word. In a less time-consuming activity, students could utilize a camera to take a picture that illustrates the vocabulary word or use a paint program to complete their illustration.

Jump In Vocabulary

Overview

This strategy requires students to work in small groups to practice defining, using, and spelling vocabulary words. As they work with their partners, they take turns jumping onto words that are taped to the ground.

Step by Step

1. Prior to using the strategy, select a location in the classroom where groups of three to five students will have space to talk, move, and jump.

2. Select 10 to 15 key vocabulary terms from the unit of study and tape them to the floor in an area where students will have space to jump and move. Also tape down two sets of feet cutouts next to the vocabulary terms. Create note cards that include the vocabulary terms as well as a definition of each term.

3. Place students in groups of three to five. Larger groups may be appropriate depending on the skill level of the students, but groups can be no smaller than three students.

4. Each group should designate one student as the "caller," while the other students line up behind the feet cutouts that have been taped on the floor.

5. The student who is calling out the words selects one of the cards and reads the definition or describes the term.

6. When the students who are standing on the feet cutouts can match the term that is taped on the floor with what is being described by the caller, they jump on that word.

7. The caller then determines if the student is correct.

8. The student who correctly jumps on a word is given the option to stay in the game and line back up on the feet cut outs. The student who did not jump on the correct term (or did not jump on the correct term in time) goes to the back of the line. The student who correctly jumps could also choose to become the caller.

Tips and Variations

- Many teachers opt to use plastic page protectors taped to the floor. Leave one slot open on the page protectors to exchange the vocabulary words.

- Ensure that students are provided with an appropriate model and explanation of how the strategy is to be used including what to do in the case there is a tie or a disagreement, or if students accidentally jump into each other.

- **Differentiation Connection**: This game can be easily differentiated beyond simple terms and definitions. Students could be asked to use the term in a sentence or to make a statement that shows they know more than just the standard definition. They could also be required to state a synonym, or an antonym.

■ Overview

Main ideas are like magnets. They attract details, they make connections between big ideas and those details, and they help to bring an understanding of themes, concepts, and ideas. This strategy uses magnet words to help students develop an understanding of vocabulary terms as well as main ideas.

■ Step by Step

1. Prior to the lesson, review the text or reading materials that will be provided to students with the goal of identifying several "magnet" words, phrases, terms, or concepts that are essential to the learning objective.

2. Provide students with a list of the "magnet" words and explain that these words are particularly important to understanding the main ideas of the text. In other words, if students do not truly understand these words, they run the risk of misunderstanding the main idea(s) in the text.

3. Provide students with one sticky note (or index card) per magnet word.

4. Prompt students to write each magnet word in the center of a sticky note.

5. As students read the lesson, they write related words, phrases, ideas, concepts, or images that surround each magnet word. Model this process for students showing them how the author elected to bundle certain ideas, details, or examples together in order to express an idea.

6. Once they are finished reading the text and have completed their sticky notes, ask them to write a sentence on the back of the sticky note. This sentence should focus on the magnet word and use, as much as possible, the words and phrases they listed on the front of their sticky note.

■ Tips and Variations

♦ *Magnet Words* are complimented by academic talk; ask students to talk with partners or share in small groups the words, phrases, and ideas they included on their sticky note. In this way, they may "cheat" off each other and write additional words or phrases they may not have on their sticky note.

♦ Depending on the magnet words selected, students may be able to combine their magnet word sentences to create a summary of the text.

♦ **Differentiation Connection**: One option is to provide different students with different magnet words to focus on during the reading of the text. Another variation is to provide the same magnet words to all students, but provide them with different texts to read.

■ Overview

This strategy requires students to analyze the use of vocabulary terms by considering examples and "non-examples." It will stretch their understanding of the word because they will have to understand the meaning and use of the word well enough to differentiate between the word being used appropriately and inappropriately.

■ Step by Step

1. Present students with a vocabulary word, such as a *Word of the Day*, and tell them that you will show several examples of the word being used. Their job will be to consider which of the examples are correct and which are incorrect.

2. Provide students with four examples of the use of the vocabulary term—two of them being correct examples, two being incorrect examples. The examples could be in the form of sentences, lists of synonyms, or images.

3. Place students in small groups of three to four and ask them to guess or select which examples are correct and which are not. Ask students to explain the reasoning for their selections.

4. If appropriate, ask groups to share their selections with the whole class.

5. Reveal the correct and incorrect answers and provide explanations for each.

■ Tips and Variations

♦ Some teachers wonder about the wisdom of providing non-examples as students learn new words. As long as students receive immediate feedback about their selections, along with a clear positive example, they will actually remember the words better than if they had completed a traditional activity like dictionary work.

♦ When evaluating student writing, you may see patterns of incorrect use of a term, word, or idea. Use this strategy to pull actual examples from student writing making sure to remove student names from the examples. In addition, rewrite the sentences on index cards or type them to be displayed for the class so no one can identify the writer(s) by their handwriting.

♦ **Technology Connection**: We sometimes rely too heavily on the grammar and spell check built into word processing programs. Select examples and non-examples that the grammar check does not catch to make students aware of the need to carefully proofread.

■ Overview

This strategy, meant to be used with small groups, utilizes a jar or container as a novel way to have students interact with the words.

■ Step by Step

1. As you prepare a lesson, select words, phrases, or terms that you'd like students to review.

2. Prepare slips of paper with the words you've selected—one word per slip of paper. Fold and place the slips of paper inside a jar. You'll need a container for each group.

3. Place students into groups of three to five and provide each group with a jar.

4. Model for students how to take turns drawing a slip of paper out of the jar. When a student selects a slip of paper, they are required to do one of the following: define the word, use it in a sentence, provide a non-example, state an antonym, and so on.

5. The other students in the group listen, elaborate, or correct what was said about the word.

6. The next student in the group then draws a slip from the jar and the process repeats until all words have been drawn out of the jar.

7. If a student who draws the word cannot define or use it, they can place the word back in the jar and draw again. If students do this, they need to pay close attention when the word is drawn by another student and defined or used.

■ Tips and Variations

♦ Rather than using this strategy only for one lesson or unit, consider using the *Word Jar* to review concepts and terms from previous weeks or from an entire quarter or semester.

♦ Some teachers opt to use this strategy as a centers-based activity. In that case, only one jar or container is needed.

♦ This strategy can be paired with *Wear a Word*. In this case, the student would pull a word from the jar and wear that word the remainder of the day.

♦ **Differentiation Connection**: Different jars can be created for different groups. This would provide specific students the opportunity to practice using the words they struggle with rather than all students practicing the same set of words.

Word of the Day

■ Overview

Just as it sounds, this strategy calls for the class to focus on one word for the day. The selected *Word of the Day* should be an essential term, phrase, or idea that will be repeated throughout the day or period.

■ Step by Step

1. As you prepare for the lesson, select a word, phrase, term, or concept that is critical for all students to know and understand.

2. Tell students that you have selected a word that is really important for everyone to know and understand.

3. Provide students with the definition of the word and an example of its use. Tell students that you'll be using the word throughout the day and that their job is to recognize when it is used. Say something like, "Students, I have selected a word that I want to make sure everyone understands. We are going to call this the *Word of the Day*. When you hear me, or someone else, use that word you are going to give a thumbs up indicating that you heard the word."

4. Use the word throughout the day, point it out while reading, use it in writing, and encourage students to use it often. You may even choose to pair it with *Wear a Word*.

5. Each day, post the *Word of the Day* in a conspicuous location—possibly on your door or on a bulletin board.

■ Tips and Variations

♦ There are many ways that students can show that they heard the word: tally marks, raised hand, noting the time on a sheet of paper, and so on.

♦ A *Word of the Day* does not actually have to be a *single* word. It can be a concept, phrase, or big idea.

♦ Create a bulletin board or word wall that contains the words that have been used throughout the year. Periodically refer to the accumulation of words to help students review concepts or find words to use during their discussions or writing tasks.

♦ Tell your co-workers, administrators, or parent volunteers about the *Word of the Day* and ask them to use the word as they interact with your students.

Part Seven

Writing

Key Idea: *The process of writing* is *the process of thinking. Allowing students an opportunity to invest and engage with topics via "writing to learn" strategies deepens content knowledge, allows for reflection, and leads to better long-term memory.*

Imagine this: you receive an email from a colleague regarding an upcoming event and your participation and responsibilities in that event. The email has a certain tone about it and is chock full of loaded pronouns, bolded words, deadlines, and questions that read a lot like accusations. Despite an occasional "smiley face" emoticon and a perfunctory "thank you" at the end of the message, you feel an irritation rising from within. Your internal filter reminds you that it is best not to respond to the email while you are irritated, so you give some thought as to the best way to respond. You know that you need to respond, but the exact words and best approach escapes you. You have a general sense of the message you want to send, but you can't quite figure out how to say it. After some thought, you sit down at your computer and begin typing. While drafting your response, things gradually begin to fall into place. The process of writing your response provides clarity on things like word choice, length, sentence structure, and overall message. You rewrite certain sentences, you copy and paste sentences to make them flow better, and you even right-click on certain words to check for more appropriate synonyms. You edit and re-read until you are satisfied that your email is appropriate, professional, and delivers the intended message.

What wasn't clear before sitting down at the computer became clear during the process of drafting and editing the email. This example illustrates the power of writing as thinking. It was during the process of writing, drafting, and editing that the message went from a vague idea to a clear, logical, and concrete response that delivered the intended message. The process of writing the email provided an opportunity to think, analyze, expand, and connect ideas. In short, the process of writing *produced* clear thinking. In this case, as is the case with writing strategies we describe in this chapter, writing serves as a tool to deepen, extend, and clarify thinking.

We fear that too often students have serious misconceptions about writing. Some students think that writing is simply the act of putting ideas down on paper or on a computer. Their misconception may be something like this: I have a clear and coherent thought—the thoughts and ideas floating around in my head are concise, intelligent, and accurate and the process of writing is simply taking those clear ideas and translating them into a written form. As illustrated by the example above, the ideas floating around in our heads are rarely 100 percent clear. Rather, the process of writing, in most cases, produces clearer ideas, more coherent thoughts, and more connected thinking.

The strategies and techniques outlined in this section focus on *writing to learn* as opposed to *learning to write*. When children are young, starting in preschool, we teach them how to write—we show them how to hold a pencil and form letters, and we begin to teach them about basic punctuation and sentence formation. While it can be argued that learning how to write is a life-long endeavor, what often gets overlooked is the power of writing to learn. Sometimes referred to as "writing for learning," this approach uses the power of writing to unleash student engagement, long-term memory, collaboration, and feedback. In the words of the National Commission on Writing (2006), the strategies and ideas we outline in this section utilize "writing in the service of learning."

Before you utilize the strategies described here, it is important to take a few moments to become acquainted with some research, background, and concepts related to writing to learn. This is particularly important for those of you who don't consider yourself "writing" teachers. Consider just some of what we know about the power of writing to learn:

- Writing supports the development of higher processing skills such as transfer of knowledge, analysis, prediction, evaluation, and conceptual thinking (Willis, 2011).

- Ten minutes of free writing before an exam or test increased test scores by 15 percent compared to students who did not write before a test (Bielock, 2011).

- Writing to learn provides a genuine purpose for writing. When writing tasks have purpose, they increase student motivation and lead to more writing (Ray, 2002).

- Of the commonly cited twenty-first-century skills so desired by colleges and employers, oral and written communication is a priority (Wagner, 2012).

- Writing utilizes the brain's executive function skills such as sequencing, planning, and organizing. In fact, of all the things students are asked to do in school, writing may be one of the most challenging executive function tasks (Cooper-Kahn & Foster, 2013).

- Writing to learn requires the retrieval of memories, elaboration of knowledge, generation of new ideas, and the creation of associations between concepts (Brown, Roediger, & McDaniel, 2014).

- Writing to learn provides teachers with three key pieces of information: what do students know, what do they still need to know, and what are they confused about (Fisher & Frey, 2007)

- Tracy Tokuhama-Espinosa, author of the 2011 book *Mind, Brain, and Education Science*, summed it up well when she said, "Written language, for example, uses more parts of the brain simultaneously than perhaps any other mental task."

- Quite simply—writing works! When students write regularly in content area classes, comprehension improves, grades increase, and standardized test scores increase (Graham & Hebert, 2010).

As you consider how to best utilize writing strategies in your own practice, it is important to note there are only three reasons we write anything: to process something, to remember something, or to say something. Of course, sometimes writing serves more than one of those purposes. As illustrated at the beginning of the chapter, responding to that email served both to process thoughts and to say something. The strategies and techniques in this chapter can also serve one or more of those purposes. For example, a *Ticket Out the Door* can provide students an opportunity to process their ideas and to communicate their knowledge to others.

One final note: all the strategies described in this chapter are considered low-stakes. We are all familiar with high-stakes writing; essay tests, college entrance exams, and research papers too often dominate the discussions of writing in school. However, low-stakes writing to learn strategies should not be overlooked. Low-stakes writing is exactly what it sounds like—low pressure, typically ungraded, and used in the development of learning rather than the assessment of it.

◼ Overview

Typically done at the end of a lesson, *3-2-1* is a short, focused *writing to learn* strategy in which students are given a chance to process what was presented during a reading, class discussion, video, or mini-lecture.

◼ Step by Step

1. Ask students to take out an index card or a scrap piece of paper. Instruct them to write a three at the top, a two in the middle, and a one on the back. Let them know they will be writing six sentences in total.

2. Give students some time to think and reflect upon what was learned during the lesson. If appropriate, prompt them with specific questions or phrases such as, "Let's take a moment to think about what we've just learned from the video. The video showed several examples of the effects of pollution on native fish species. Take a minute to think about what we learned and why it was important."

3. Next to the three on their cards, they will write three details from the lesson that they think are most important to remember. Details could include: key words, names of people or places, events, or descriptions.

4. Next to the two on their cards, students will write two reasons why the content relates personally to them. This could include examples they thought were emotional or memorable, action items they might be able to take, or connections to the real world.

5. Next to the one on their cards, students will write a question they have about what was learned. This could be something they do not understand, something they want to know more about, or something they are simply curious about.

6. Collect the cards as a ticket out the door and spend time prior to the next lesson reviewing the cards for any misconceptions, personal connections, and questions posed by the students. Use this information to re-teach misunderstood concepts or to provide enrichment opportunities.

◼ Tips and Variations

♦ As with many strategies, it is important to model this process for students, particularly the first time it is used. In other words, get up in front of students and conduct a think aloud showing students the connections and questions you made.

♦ Consider using *3-2-1* cards as *Focal Points* and prompt your students with specific questions in order to have an academic discussion.

♦ **Differentiation Connection**: For students that may struggle, consider providing them with sentences starters or very specific questions to answer.

■ Overview

The typical classroom writing task involves students creating a written work for one specific audience—the teacher. This strategy provides students the opportunity to reflect on their learning and knowledge by creating a written product, such as a summary or a story, for a different audience.

■ Step by Step

1. Remind students of the objectives of the lesson or unit.

2. Provide them with time to review materials, resources, notes, or previous classwork with the goal of getting a clear understanding of what they have learned about the topic.

3. Tell students that they'll be given some time to write a summary, story, fact sheet, blog entry, etc., that accurately reflects the concepts and ideas that they've been studying.

4. Before students begin writing tell them that this writing task will be a bit different. Instead of the only audience being the teacher, tell them that their writing will be given to and read by another group of people. For example, when studying a physics concept like motion and force, tell students that you have arranged for their papers to be read by a group of college students who are studying engineering.

5. Provide time for students to create their written works for the identified audience.

6. Provide feedback and direction throughout the process, reminding students that their work will be read by other adults. In other words, the "classwork" is going to be leaving the classroom.

■ Tips and Variations

♦ An audience, particularly one that students value, provides a genuine reason to engage in the writing task. For example, if students know that their writing will be read by other adults and parents during a family night, they'll likely have additional incentive (beyond a grade) to create a polished piece of writing.

♦ Altered audiences do not always have to consist of adults. In fact, there is tremendous value in asking students to summarize their understanding of a topic for an audience that does not have the same background or experience. For example, asking eighth grade students to condense the main ideas of a novel like Ender's Game for a group of fifth grade students requires that they be succinct and use age-appropriate vocabulary when they are writing.

♦ For creative writing tasks, such as short stories and poems, some teachers have found success by distributing the students' work to local doctors' offices and having them placed in waiting rooms along with magazines and flyers.

Overview

This strategy offers students a chance to develop their own ideas and connections to the content while gathering feedback and additional ideas from their peers. As a *writing to learn* strategy that utilizes small groups of three or four students, it provides a framework for students to list their own content knowledge and to work with their peers to expand their knowledge.

Step by Step

1. Give each student a half sheet of paper or a note card, or designate a place in a notebook for five to seven sentences.

2. Remind students of the objective of the lesson and provide them some think time to reflect on what they've been learning. If needed, provide students with time to review any notes, books, or materials that they have been utilizing during the learning.

3. Ask students to write one statement that describes something they know about the focus of the lesson. For example, the student may write, "When conducting a scientific experiment, the first step is to determine a question to investigate."

4. Once students have written their statement, ask them to hand the paper to another person in their group.

5. When students receive another student's paper, they read and respond to what was written. Without talking, students add to the ideas on the paper. Those comments could be in the form of questions, agreement statements, or additional facts and details. For example, a student might add the following to the sentence in Step 3: "The second step is to determine the best method for conducting the experiment."

6. Students continue to trade papers and add ideas until all partners have *Expanded the Sentences* of all other students in their small group.

7. Once students receive their original paper back, guide them to read the comments from their peers and to use those ideas to expand, revise, or edit their original writing.

Tips and Variations

- During Step 3, rather than giving broad, open-ended questions for the focus of the writing, many students will benefit from specific sentence starters or prompts to begin their writing.

- **Critical Thinking Connection**: Knowing that students should be assessing their own understanding, once they read the comments from their peers, lead them to answer such questions as, "Which comments made you re-think something you had written?" or "In what ways is your understanding clearer now that you have read the ideas from your classmates?"

■ Overview

This strategy challenges students to write about a specific topic, non-stop, for a short period of time, recognizing that sometimes we just need to begin writing before we have a clear understanding of what we want to say.

■ Step by Step

1. Ask students to get out a sheet of paper.

2. Remind them of the lesson objective, including main ideas, examples, or definitions.

3. Tell students that they will be writing for exactly 3 minutes without stopping. Tell them that this may be difficult but their job is to continuously write for the entire 3 minutes. If they get stuck, tell them to write, "I can't think of anything to write about."

4. Give students a question, prompt, or a sentence starter and provide them with some think time.

5. Set a timer for 3 minutes and instruct students to begin writing.

6. Once the timer goes off, ask students to finish their last thought or idea.

7. If appropriate, allow students the chance to share their ideas and thoughts with partners.

■ Tips and Variations

♦ The first time this strategy is used, it may be wise to give students a topic they have interest in or in which they have some background. For example, ask students to write non-stop for 3 minutes about their favorite game or a time when they had a lot of fun.

♦ When the timer is going and students are *Fast Writing*, tell them not to worry about grammar, spelling, editing, and so on. Their task is to simply get ideas down on paper.

♦ **Differentiation Connection**: There are two easy ways to adjust this strategy based on the needs of your students: First, adjust the amount of time they are asked to write. Second, provide students with specific words, phrases, or ideas to include. In this case, students can refer to a *Key Word List* or look at an *Anchor*.

■ Overview

On the surface, a summary consisting of one, single word might seem simple. In reality, the act of being succinct is much more challenging than it seems. This strategy calls for students to consider what they've learned about a concept and then to condense that learning down to a singular word.

■ Step by Step

1. Provide students with an index card.

2. On the front of the card, prompt students to brainstorm and list the words, phrases, or concepts that pertain to the lesson. Say something like, "Students, I want you to close your eyes for a moment and think about all the words that seem important from today's lesson. Think about important words or phrases. Think about words that can describe what we've learned. Think about words you may have heard repeated a couple of times."

3. Provide time for students to list their words on the front of their card.

4. After students have listed the key terms, instruct them to select one word (or one phrase, if appropriate) that accurately reflects the ideas and concepts that they learned. Ask them to write that one word on the other side of their index card.

5. Once students have completed both sides of their index cards, lead students to have a partner or small group discussion requiring that they provide a rationale for their *One-Word Summary*. During this time, students not only share their words but they tell *why* they selected that word.

6. At the end of the lesson, collect the cards and review for commonalities and insights.

■ Tips and Variations

♦ The *One-Word Summary* is powerful for two reasons: First, the process of selecting a singular word requires that students think about, reflect, designate, analyze, and (possibly) change their minds. Reviewing all the words from the brainstorm requires students to be thoughtful about their selection. Second, students have to provide a rationale for their selection *and* they have to share that rationale with a peer. This requires that students verbalize their thinking and can lead to additional insights by the students.

♦ Some teachers have asked if the *One-Word Summary* can ever be more than *one* word. The simple answer is yes, but we encourage teachers to limit the summary to, at most, three words. Again, part of the effectiveness of this strategy is the reflection and analysis it requires of students. If they are allowed too many options, they may not critically think about their selections.

♦ **Technology Connection:** After collecting the *One-Word Summaries*, create a word cloud to highlight all the words chosen by the students. In word clouds, the words repeated most often will appear in the largest font. Three great resources for word clouds are:

  www.wordle.net
  www.abcya.com
  www.tagul.com

■ Overview

Response Journals provide students a place to write reflections, summarize their learning, and make personal connections to the content being learned. They also provide a substantive way for teachers to provide feedback to students.

■ Step by Step

1. *Response Journals* are typically composition books or spiral-bound notebooks that students can use throughout the semester or the year. Each student should have their own journal.

2. At the end of a lesson, the end of a class, or other appropriate times where students need to stop and process their learning, prompt them to locate their journals.

3. Provide students with an open-ended question or prompt and give them time to write a response. Remind students that you'll be reading the journals and will be providing a response to the ideas they've written.

4. Give students 5 to 10 minutes to write a response. Ask them to dig deep into the content to make applications of the knowledge, to ask questions, and to think about how they might apply the knowledge.

5. Collect the journals and set aside an appropriate time to read student entries and provide a response to what they've written. What differentiates this strategy from a typical journal is that the teacher responds to the student writing. It only becomes a *Response Journal* once the teacher provides a response.

■ Tips and Variations

♦ There are many writing to learn strategies that can be completed inside of the *Response Journals*: *The Week in Review, 3-2-1,* or a *One Word Summary*.

♦ Consider asking a guest reader to respond to student journal entries. Of course, if you invite another person to read student entries, make sure that students know this ahead of time. By the way, this is a great task for a parent volunteer.

♦ Finding the time to read the entries for all students in a class can be a challenge. We encourage teachers to carefully plan when to use them. If they are used daily, it will be nearly impossible to read and respond to every student. Providing substantive feedback takes time.

♦ **Technology Connection**: If you are in a technology-rich environment, you may choose to use an ongoing shared Google Doc or a Microsoft OneNote Notebook for the *Response Journal*. If so, use a note feature or turn the font to a different color so your feedback stands out from the student's original writing.

■ Overview

Just as many newspapers provide a week in review that highlights the major news stories or articles of interest for its readers, this strategy provides students a chance to consider the major learning, accomplishments, or memorable events from the week.

■ Step by Step

1. Ask students to get out a sheet of paper or to locate their *Response Journals*.

2. Prompt students to consider all the content, ideas, tasks, or projects that have been a part of the past week. If appropriate, allow them to look through notes, materials, or resources.

3. Tell students that they are going to spend some time writing about everything that was learned and accomplished during the past week.

4. Instruct students to write for 5 to 10 minutes about what they learned, what tasks they completed, and what experiences they had as it relates to the major learning objectives.

5. After students complete their *Week in Review*, have them share with partners or small groups.

6. Collect student work and analyze for insights, commonalities, and any opportunities for re-teaching or enrichment.

■ Tips and Variations

♦ Remember that, like all the strategies in this section, the *Week in Review* is *a writing to learn* strategy. As such, the focus is on the ideas, connections, and major learning. Do not focus on grammar, punctuation, and spelling. Of course, we always want students to use proper mechanics when writing, but do not use these strategies to assess those skills.

♦ Part of the power of this strategy is that it prompts students to think about both what they learned as well as what experiences they had along the way. Thinking about learning as well as the experiences or tasks that lead to that learning supports long-term memory.

♦ **Differentiation Connection**: It may be helpful, depending on the needs of your students, to provide specific prompts to help them remember what they accomplished throughout the week. For example, you might say something like, "Do you remember on Tuesday when we watched the video clip? Do you remember what the video showed us how to do? Perhaps include that in your writing."

■ Overview

We often ask students to summarize *what* they've learned, but how often do we ask them to consider the *why* behind learning it? Why something is learned, and the connections students make between the content and their personal lives, is every bit as important as what they learn. This strategy challenges students to think about what they've learned *and* why it is important.

■ Step by Step

1. At the end of a lesson or during a time when students need to stop and reflect on their learning, ask students to get out a sheet of paper.

2. Provide students with time to think about the main points of the lesson. If appropriate, allow them to refer to their notes, resources, or materials.

3. Give students 3 to 5 minutes to write about what they are learning. Say something like, "Students, we are going to take a couple of minutes to write about what we've been learning. During this time, I want you to do a brain dump, simply write down what you think is important about what we are learning. You could include facts, details, examples, definitions, etc."

4. After students spend a few minutes writing about the *what* of the learning, ask them to pause and think about *why* the information is important to remember. Prompt them with questions such as:

   "How might this information impact our community or your family?"

   "Has something like that ever happened to you?"

   "How could you use this information in the future?"

   "Does this information contradict anything you were previously taught?"

   "Why might this information be important to remember?"

5. Have students turn over their sheet of paper and write a response to the *why* prompt.

6. After students write about what they've learned and why it is important, ask them to share their ideas with a partner or small group.

■ Tips and Variations

♦ When considering *why* questions and prompts (Step 4), reflect upon the needs and unique characteristics of your students. What are the likes, dislikes, hobbies, skills, and interests of your students? When you can help connect the content to something that students are naturally interested in, the personal connections become much easier. In addition, personally relevant information aids long-term memory and recall.

♦ **Technology Connection**: Consider using *Digital Sticky Notes* to allow students to share their connections with each other. This will also allow information to be shared among a larger group of students and provides an easy way to categorize student ideas.

■ Overview

The *Write On* strategy is an example of a written conversation. Although written conversations, as an instructional technique, have been around for decades, most recently, Harvey "Smokey" Daniels, in his outstanding 2013 book *Best-Kept Teaching*, has reignited excitement and interest in written conversations as a method to engage students. This strategy offers students a chance to wrestle with their own ideas on a topic and to get feedback and additional ideas from their peers.

■ Step by Step

1. Place students in groups of three to five.

2. Provide students with a brief reminder of the objective or focus of the lesson.

3. Guide students to review any notes, books, or materials that they have been utilizing during the lesson. Provide them time to individually review those materials with the goal of summarizing and discussing their current knowledge and understanding.

4. Provide each student with a blank sheet of paper and ask them to write for approximately 2 to 4 minutes about what they know, believe, or understand about the topic.

5. When the writing time is up, instruct students to hand their paper to the person to their left.

6. When students receive another student's paper, they read and respond to what was written. Without talking, students add to the ideas on the paper. Those comments could be in the form of questions, agreement statements, or additional facts and details.

7. Students should continue to pass the papers around the group until they receive their original paper back.

8. Once students receive their original paper back, guide them to read the comments from their peers and to use those ideas to expand, revise, or edit their original writing.

■ Tips and Variations

♦   While the *Expand the Sentence* strategy prompts students to add single ideas to the work of their peers, the *Write On* strategy takes on more of a conversational tone. As such, students should be aware that conversations consist of questions, comments, and disagreements.

♦   **Differentiation Connection**: Reluctant students or struggling writers could use the peer review time to highlight key words or code the reading with symbols/icons (such as ?, !, :). Advanced students could also use the peer review time to reference external resources to double check factual information.

                                                                    Battling Boredom Part 2

■ Overview

The connection between writing and academic talk is inherent. Both are an expression of our thoughts utilizing language. This strategy recognizes this connection and provides students with an opportunity to revise their thinking after having a discussion with a partner.

■ Step by Step

1. After about 10 to 15 minutes of new content, provide students an opportunity to process what they are learning. Ask them to get out a sheet of paper.

2. Tell students that they will be writing for about 2 to 3 minutes in order to process and think about the information that was presented.

3. Provide students with time to write. If necessary, provide them with a specific prompt or question such as, "Students, please take about 2 minutes to think about the ideas that I just presented to you. Write about what seemed important or what questions you have. Or write about what terms, examples, or definitions I provided. Basically, just use this as an opportunity to write and reflect on the ideas I just shared."

4. After students complete their writing, ask them to share their ideas and thoughts with a partner or a small group. During this time, they do not have to share their actual written responses. Rather, the goal is to verbalize their thoughts and use their written responses as prompts or reminders.

5. After students share with partners, ask them to go back and re-read, review, and revise their original work. Say something like, "Students, please take about 2 more minutes to read what you previously wrote in order to revise your writing. You will not be editing in the sense that you should focus on grammar and spelling. Instead, I want you to revise for ideas. For example, was there anything that your partner said that you should add to your writing? Are there any ideas that you should delete or erase because you now realize there was a mistake?"

6. If appropriate and if time allows, offer students the chance to have another partner discussion (perhaps with a different partner) that focuses on what ideas were changed, updated, or reinforced.

■ Tips and Variations

♦ Consider combining this strategy with *Conferencing, Collaborative Sticky Notes,* or *Illustrated Vocabulary.*

♦ This strategy is an excellent way to support understanding of complex ideas or topics with nuance. For example, as a response to a text, *Write, Talk, Revise* can be focused on topics such as theme, character development, or author's purpose.

♦ **Technology Connection:** If technology is going to be used with this strategy, ensure that you utilize a "track changes" feature or make sure that students use a different font color to highlight their revisions.

Part Eight

Student Engagement Strategies that Don't Work

Introduction

Key Idea: *Although some strategies and techniques have been around for a long time, not all the "classics" are actually effective at engaging students in real, authentic ways. The following strategies should be removed from regular classroom use.*

There are some traditional "tried and true" engagement strategies used by educators that actually do the opposite—they increase the likelihood of *disengagement*. All teachers know that engagement is the key to learning, but not all strategies and techniques are created equally. The strategies we highlight here all have one thing in common—they impede, slow down, or outright stop true, authentic engagement.

Before we discuss the specific strategies that should be removed from our educational repertoire, it is important to consider the differences between true engagement and merely on-task behavior. We know that engagement is the key to learning, but we also know that many of our students are bored with the curriculum and activities being offered in classrooms. To battle this problem, much focus and attention has been placed on getting students to be "on-task." Indeed, the link between on-task behavior and student achievement is strong. However, just as an office worker can be busy without being productive, a student can be on-task without being engaged in the learning. True, long-lasting learning comes not merely as a result of being on-task, but as a result of being deeply engaged in meaningful, relevant, and important tasks.

We see examples of on-task but disengaged behavior every day: students mindlessly copying notes from a screen, listening to a lecture but daydreaming about what to do after school, or robotically completing a worksheet. Some students, particularly older ones, have become masters at what Bishop and Pflaum (2005) refer to as "pretend-attend." They've mastered the ability to look busy, focused, and on-task, but in reality they are disengaged in the actual learning.

Schlecty (2002) describes student engagement as a continuum ranging from outright rebellion to authentic engagement. True, meaningful, authentic engagement involves students being deeply immersed in work that makes sense to them and that has immediate value. Unfortunately, too many educators are satisfied with what Schlecty describes as ritual or passive compliance. Those classrooms will see kids "busy" and completing their work, but not truly engaged in work that means something to them. Unfortunately, too many educators focus so much on compliance that they sacrifice authentic engagement.

As you consider each of the strategies described here, ask yourself this very important question: *If I use this strategy, am I likely to increase or decrease authentic engagement?* We believe you'll see that they do not live up to the standards of true engagement.

Unlike the strategies described in the other chapters of this book, you'll notice that this section does not include step-by-step directions for each strategy. If we think that these strategies should be removed from your repertoire, it would not make sense for us to provide step-by-step directions.

In athletic competitions, the fastest and strongest individuals win the prize. Unfortunately, many educators assume that students who are the quickest to answer questions (or the quickest to *offer* answers) are the smartest and should be rewarded. The Academic Decathlon strategy is the practice of the teacher consistently calling on, rewarding, or granting privileges to those students who are the fastest to raise their hands, answer questions, or volunteer. While speed and automaticity with certain things like math facts are important, when seeking to engage students in deep, meaningful ways, the invitation needs to be open to all students, not just the "smart" kids who can answer questions quickly. When teachers primarily seek to engage the "best academic athletes," they send a very clear (and unfortunate) message that education, learning, and growth are for a select few individuals for whom learning comes fast and easy. Learning, engagement, and participation is not a race and we need not reward the students who are fastest or most eager to answer questions and participate.

During whole group activities such as lectures, there are times when teachers will ask questions of students in order to gauge understanding and progress. While questioning is a great way to engage students, there are times when teachers will "hunt" for a correct answer. The Answer Hunt strategy is the practice of asking a question and then calling on several students before a correct answer is found. In other words, the teacher hunts for a correct answer from students. Rather than re-framing the question or allowing extended think time or opportunities for students to talk with each other, the teacher continues to call on many students in the class until (sometimes by accident), a student answers the question correctly.

This is the classic strategy where the teacher assigns a certain part of a text or a certain portion of an assignment to each student in the class. Typically, the teacher begins by asking one student to read their part or answer their question while the other students in the class are asked to listen and wait until their turn to participate. Round Robin reading is probably the most common of the "robins"; this approach assigns each student in the class to a different portion of a text (a paragraph, for example) with each student reading their part and then supposedly following along as other students read their parts. This practice is ineffective for many reasons. Although the teacher intends that all students follow along until it is their turn, this approach typically results in students focusing only on completing *their* portion of the text. Consider the reality of what is likely happening in the minds of students—they are assigned a paragraph to read, they skip ahead and pre-read that paragraph to themselves, then they wait until it is their turn to read, and once their turn is over they breathe a sigh of relief and take a break. This approach all but guarantees that only one student will be engaged at any given time.

Many teachers have recognized the limitations of this approach and instead have implemented a strategy where reading or participation is designed to be random. "Popcorn Reading," as it has been nicknamed, is a popular approach designed to keep students focused since the order of participation is supposed to be random and unknown. During Popcorn Reading a student finishes their portion and then the student or the teacher randomly calls on another student in the class to read the next section. Although we would consent that the popcorn approach is better than a true Round Robin, it still all but guarantees that only one student will be participating at any given time. Some will argue that students need to follow along to be able to continue the reading/problem/discussion in case they get "popcorned," but we have seen many occasions where students get irritated, embarrassed, or outright mad at each other for being called on by another student. It is also likely that some students will only call on their friends to be the next to participate. In addition, in most classroom settings, once a student has been called upon to participate, they rarely get called again. So, students quickly learn that after their turn is complete, they can mentally check out.

There are times when students need to copy information, but too many teachers assume that copying—in and of itself—is an engagement strategy. It is not; copying information (such as taking notes or writing dictionary definitions) does not guarantee thinking or engagement. Copying is merely an act of compliance and a student can copy information without actually thinking about it or processing the meaning of what they are copying. Put plainly, we cannot assume that copying information will result in engagement or learning.

While copying may be necessary at times, what is most important is what students do with the information they have copied. It is also important to keep in mind that copying is not synonymous with writing. The strategies shared in the writing section of this book focus on *writing to learn*, not writing as copying.

To engage students with content that has been copied, consider the following steps:

♦ *Keep it short*—teachers should limit the amount of information that students need to copy. Remember that copying can be boring and students can get fatigued very quickly. So, consider carefully the most important content or concepts that students need to master and have them only copy small amounts of the most essential information. Tell students why the information is important and discuss those key ideas both before and after they have copied it.

♦ *Discuss it*—refer to the many strategies in the "Academic Talk" and "Questioning" sections of this book for methods to get students to discuss and elaborate on what they have copied.

♦ *Rewrite it*—once students have copied information and heard directly from the teacher about why it is important, they should talk about the information and then rewrite, rephrase, or summarize their understanding of the content.

Lectures are so ubiquitous—so widely used as an instructional strategy—that many educators assume it is effective. While many researchers and educators have offered excellent strategies to make lectures more engaging, it is our belief that shorter, mini-lectures are most effective. One needs only to look to the research on attention span, the role of emotions in learning, or the negative effects of sitting still for long periods of time to realize that long lectures are not good for learning. In order to make lectures more effective, make them shorter and practice the strategies and methods outlined in the various sections of this book.

One final challenge for lectures as an instructional method: lectures are often the default method by many secondary teachers (as well as those in higher education) because they feel that there is too much material to cover in class. This is certainly one of the failings of the standards movement, as teachers are often given more standards/content to teach than is realistic given their number of days or weeks in their course. This has practically demanded that teachers go "a mile wide and an inch deep." While an extended, long-winded lecture will allow the teacher to say that they have covered material, there is little likelihood that students will have actually learned it. As educators, our job is not to "cover" the standards, it is to ensure that students learn the standards. Since our job is to ensure that they learn, we need to utilize those techniques that increase the likelihood of their engagement. And extended lectures do not accomplish that.

This has long been a favorite of some teachers who desire to catch students off guard when they think they are not paying attention or appropriately participating. It often looks something like this—the teacher is lecturing or asking questions of the whole group when they spy a student who they believe is off-task or behaving inappropriately. Believing that embarrassment is a good thing and that students need to be put in their place, they call on the student by saying something like, "Ethan! I was just explaining to the class one of the postulates you need to know for the test. Since you were talking, I assume you know all the answers. Tell the class the definition since you seem to know everything." Obviously, such an approach is not good for kids and not conducive to a productive learning environment. In addition, this approach almost always backfires because it pits students against their teachers in an adversarial environment.

Perhaps one of the most challenging habits to break is the practice of beginning a question or a prompt with a student's name. Many educators are in the habit of saying something like, "Bromley, what is the result of your group's experiment" or "Hunter, share with the class how you solved question 12." The problem with this approach is that it signals to the rest of the class that their engagement and participation is not necessary. The student who is called upon is highly engaged, but the rest of the students often tune out. While the teacher expects that all the other students listen and follow along, the reality is that most students who are "off the hook" at that moment occupy their minds with other thoughts.

The following suggestions and changes will help to overcome the habit of Name First:

♦ *Signal* to the class that you want everyone to think about the question or prompt.

♦ Pose the question or the prompt followed by appropriate *think time/wait time.*

♦ If an individual student needs to be called upon, place their *name at the end* of the question after the wait time has been given:

> Students, I am going to pose a question that I want everyone to think about. This is an important question because it will provide the basis for our discussion and activities today (*signal*). Yesterday, we discussed the role of conflict in understanding why Jem, Scout, and Del made assumptions about Boo Radley. I want everyone to think about this for a moment (*think time/wait time*). Allie, would you share your thoughts with us (*name*)?

By definition, a rhetorical question is one that requires no answer. There are times when lecturers, speakers, or writers will use rhetorical questions as a literary device to make a point or to highlight an issue. Often, they are used as a humorous way to emphasize something or to show how there is common agreement among the group. Notice that rhetorical questions are most commonly used during scenarios where there is no expected interaction between the person asking the question and the audience. Since these types of questions require no answer on the part of the students, they also require no thinking or engagement. As a result, they should be eliminated as a classroom strategy. If you find yourself in the habit of using a lot of rhetorical questions, consider making a few adjustments. First, tell your students at the outset that the question is rhetorical—that they need not answer the question because the answer is designed to be obvious. That obvious answer, by the way, typically only requires a simple yes or no response —"Everyone would love to get an A in this class, right?" Then follow up by telling your students that you do want them to think about and talk about something related to that first question. It might sound like this,

> Everyone would love to get an A in this class, right? That's a rhetorical question, I don't expect an answer. But there is something I would like you all to think about. What does an A really mean? If you get an A in my class, what does that prove? Is an A in my class worth more than an A in another teacher's class? I want you to think about this for a moment. In just a minute, you are going to share your ideas with the people at your table.

Another difficult habit to break is making some of the participation in classroom activities an optional thing. Teachers are encouraged to make learning and participation mandatory for all students (as it should be), but we sometimes inadvertently send messages that participation is voluntary. Typically done during whole group settings, Who Wants to ...? is when the teacher asks a question or gives a prompt that starts with something like, "Who wants to ...", "Who would like to ...", or "Who is willing to ..." When teachers begin questions by asking for volunteers, it allows students the chance to opt out. In addition, if we are honest, we know that most classrooms have a few students that volunteer for almost everything and a lot of students who do not volunteer for anything. Effective teachers almost never ask for volunteers. Rather, they seek to engage as many students at a time as possible. While there certainly may be some occasions where asking for a volunteer is appropriate, those times should be limited and rare.

References

Bauman, J., & Kame'enui, E. (2012). *Vocabulary Instruction: Research to Practice*. New York: The Guilford Press.

Beck, I., McKeown, M., & Kucan, L. (2013). *Bringing Words to Life*. New York: The Guilford Press.

Bellebaum, C., & Daum, L. (2007). Cerebral Involvement in Executive Control. Retrieved from www.ncbi.nlm.nih.gov/pubmed/17786814.

Bielock, S. (2011). *Choke: What the Secrets of the Brain Reveal about Getting It Right When You Have To*. Washington, DC: Free Press.

Bill and Melinda Gates Foundation. (2015). *Teachers Know Best: Making Data Work for Teachers and Students*. Retrieved from www.gatesfoundation.org/.

Bishop, P. A., & Pflaum, S. W. (2005). Student Perceptions of Action, Relevance, and Pace. *Middle School Journal*. 36 (4): 1–12.

Blatt-Gross, C. (2015). Why Do We Make Students Sit Still in Class? Retrieved from www.cnn.com/2014/03/30/living/no-sitting-still-movement-schools/.

Brenner, L. (2015). 3 Ways to Increase Student Engagement in Your Classroom. Retrieved from www.iste.org/explore/articleDetail?articleid=590&category=Innovator-solutions&article=.

Britton, A., & Shipley, M. (2010). Bored to Death? *International Journal of Epidemiology*. 39 (2): 370–371.

Bromley, K. (2007). Nine Things Every Teacher Should Know about Words and Vocabulary Instruction. *Journal of Adolescent and Adult Literacy*. 50 (7): 528–537.

Brown, P., Roediger, H., & McDaniel, M. (2014). *Make It Stick: The Science of Successful Learning*. Cambridge, MA: Harvard University Press.

Chaddock-Heyman, L., Erickson, K. I., Holtrop, J. I., Voss, M. W., Pontifex, M. B., Raine, L. B., Hillman, C. H., & Kramer, A. F. (2014). Aerobic Fitness Is Associated with Greater White Matter Integrity in Children. Retrieved from www.ncbi.nlm.nih.gov/pmc/articles/PMC4137385/.

Coe, D. P., Pivarnik, J. M., Womack, C. J., Reeves, M. J., & Malina, R. M. (2006) Effect of Physical Education and Activity Levels on Academic Achievement in Children. *Medicine and Science in Sports and Exercise*. 38 (8): 1515–1519.

Collins, R. (2013). Using Captions to Reduce Barriers to Native American Student Success. *American Indian Culture and Research Journal.* 37 (3): 75–86.

Cooper-Kahn, J., & Foster, M. (2013). *Boosting Executive Skills in the Classroom: A Practical Guide for Educators.* San Francisco, CA: Jossey-Bass.

Daniels, H. (2013). *The Best-Kept Teaching Secret: How Written Conversations Engage Kids, Activate Learning, Grow Fluent Writers … K-12.* Thousand Oaks, CA: Corwin Press.

Daniels, L. (2009). A Longitudinal Analysis of Achievement Goals: From Affective Antecedents to Emotional Effects and Achievement Outcomes. *Journal of Educational Psychology.* 101 (4): 948–963.

Daniels, L., & Tze, V. (2014). How Do Teachers Want Students to Cope with Boredom? *ASCD Express.* 9 (8).

Darling-Hammond, L., Zielezinski, M. B., & Goldman, S. (2014). *Using Technology to Support At-Risk Students' Learning* (Rep.). Retrieved from https://edpolicy.stanford.edu/publications/pubs/1241.

Dewar, M., Alber, J., Butler, C., Cowan, N., & Della Sala, S. (2012). Brief Wakeful Resting Boosts New Memories Over the Long Term. Retrieved from http://journals.sagepub.com/doi/abs/10.1177/0956797612441220.

Dornhecker, M., Blake, J. J., Benden, M., & Wendel, M. L. (2015). The Effect of Stand-Biased Desks on Academic Engagement: An Exploratory Study. *International Journal of Health Promotion and Education.* 53 (5): 1–10.

Ferrera, K., Golinkoff, R. M., Hirsh-Pasek, K., Lam, W., & Newcombe, N. S. (2011). Block Talk: Spatial Language during Block Play. *Mind, Brain, and Education.* 5 (3): 143–151.

Fisher, D., Frey, N., & Pumpian, I. (2012). *How to Create a Culture of Achievement.* Alexandria, VA: ASCD.

Gallup. (2012). The School Cliff: Student Engagement Drops with Each School Year. Retrieved from www.gallup.com/opinion/gallup/170525/school-cliff-student-engagement-drops school-year.aspx.

Gallup. (2013). What Americans Said about the American Schools. Retrieved from http://pdkpoll2015.pdkintl.org/wp-content/uploads/2015/08/pdkpoll45_2013.pdf.

Gallup. (2015). Gallup Student Poll – Engaged Today, Ready for Tomorrow. Retrieved from www.gallup.com/services/189926/student-poll-2015-results.aspx.

Graham, S. & Hebert, M. (2010). *Writing to Read.* A Report from Carnegie Corporation of New York.

Harris, B. (2010). *Battling Boredom.* New York: Routledge.

Harris, B. (2014). *Creating a Classroom Culture that Supports the Common Core.* New York: Routledge.

Hart, T., & Risely, B. (1995). *Meaningful Differences in the Everyday Experience of Young American Children.* Baltimiore, MD: Paul H. Brookes Publishing Co.

Hart, W., & Albarracin, D. (2009). The Effects of Chronic Achievement Motivation and Achievement Primes on the Activation of Achievement and Fun Goals. *Journal of Personality and Social Psychology.* 97 (6): 1129–1141.

Hattie, J. (2009). *Visible Learning*. New York: Routledge.

Herold, B. (2016, June 06). What It Takes to Move from 'Passive' to 'Active' Tech Use in K-12 Schools. *Education Week*. 35 (35). Retrieved from www.edweek.org/ew/articles/2016/06/09/what-it-takes-to-move-from-passive.html?qs=technology%2Bstudent%2Bengagement%2Binmeta%3ACover_year%3D2016%2Binmeta%3Agsaentity_Source%2520URL%2520entities%3DEducation%2520Week%2520Articles.

Jarrett, O. (2013). A Research-Based Case for Recess. Retrieved from www.playworks.org/sites/default/files/US-play-coalition_Research-based-case-forrecess.pdf.

Jensen, E. (2013). *Engaging Students with Poverty in Mind*. Alexandria, VA: ASCD.

Katja, M., Macedona, M., & Kriegstein, K. (2015). Visual and Motor Cortices Differentially Support the Translation of Foreign Language Words. Retrieved from www.sciencedirect.com/science/article/pii/S0960982214015693.

Kuntz, B. (2012, June). Engage Students by Embracing Technology. *Education Update*. 54 (6). Retrieved from www.ascd.org/publications/newsletters/education-update/jun12/vol54/num06/Engage-Students-by-Embracing-Technology.aspx.

Marzano, R., Pickering, D., & Pollack, J. (2001). *Classroom Instruction That Works: Research-Based Strategies for Increasing Student Achievement*. Alexandria, VA: ASCD.

McKeown, M., Beck, I. L., Omanson, R. C., & Pople, M. T. (1985). Some Effects of the Nature and Frequency of Vocabulary Instruction on the Knowledge and Use of Words. *Reading Research Quarterly*. 20 (5): 522–535.

National Commission on Writing. (2006). Writing and School Reform. Retrieved from www.collegeboard.com/prod_downloads/writingcom/writing-school-reform-natl-commwriting.pdf.

National Institute of Child Health and Human Development. (2000). Teaching Children to Read: An Evidence-Based Assessment of the Scientific Research Literature on Reading and Its Implications for Reading Instruction. Retrieved from www.nichd.nih.gov/publications/pubs/nrp/Pages/smallbook.aspx.

Nestojko, J., Bui, D. C., Kornell, N., & Bjork, E. L. (2014). Expecting to Teach Enhances Learning and Organization of Knowledge in Free Recall of Text Passages. *Memory and Cognition*. 42 (7): 1038–1048.

Padak, N., Bromley, K., Rasinski, T., & Newton, E. (2012). Vocabulary: Five Common Misconceptions. *Educational Leadership Online*. Vol. 69.

Parasuraman, R., & Jiang, Y. (2012). Individual Differences in Cognition, Affect, and Performance: Behavioral, Neuroimaging, and Molecular Genetic Approaches. *Neuroimage*. 59 (1): 70–82.

Rasinki, T. (2012). *Why Reading Fluency Should Be Hot!* Hoboken, NJ: John Wiley and Sons.

Ratey, J. (2008). *Spark: The Revolutionary Science of Exercise and the Brain*. Boston, MA: Little Brown & Co.

Rutherford, P. (2009). *Why Didn't I Learn This in College?* Alexandria, VA: Just Ask Publications

Sarver, D. E., Rapport, M. D., Kofler, M. J., Raiker, J. S., & Friedman, L. M. (2015). Hyperactivity in Attention-Deficit/Hyperactivity Disorder (ADHD): Impairing Deficit or Compensatory Behavior? *Journal of Abnormal Child Psychology*. 43: 1219–1232.

Schlecty, P. C. (2002). *Working on the Work: An Action Plan for Teachers, Principals, and Superintendents*. San Francisco, CA: Jossey-Bass Education Series.

Schmidt, M., Benzing,V., & Kramer, M. (2016). Classroom-Based Physical Activity Breaks and Children's Attention: Cognitive Engagement Works! Retrieved from http://journal.frontiersin.org/article/10.3389/fpsyg.2016.01474/full.

Sheninger, E. (2015, March 08). Engagement Does Not Always Equate Learning [Web log post]. Retrieved from www.http://esheninger.blogspot.com/2015/03/engagement-does-not-always-equate-to.html.

Teychenne, M., Costigan, S. A., & Parker, K. (2015). The Association Between Sedentary Behaviour and Risk of Anxiety: A Systematic Review. Retrieved from http://bmcpublichealth.biomedcentral.com/articles/10.1186/s12889-015-1843-x.

Tine, M. (2014) Acute Aerobic Exercise: An Intervention for the Selective Visual Attention and Reading Comprehension of Low-Income Adolescents. *Frontiers in Psychology*. 5: 575.

Tokuhama-Espinosa, T. (2011). *Mind, Brain, and Education Science*. New York: Norton Press.

Vogel-Walcutt, J., Fiorella, L., Carper, T., & Schatz, S. (2012). The Definition, Assessment, and Mitigation of State Boredom Within Educational Settings: A Comprehensive Review. *Educational Psychology Review*. 24 (1): 89–111.

Walsh, J., & Sattes, B. (2017). *Quality Questioning*. Thousand Oaks, CA: Corwin Press

Wiggins, G., & McTighe, J. (2005). *Understanding by Design*. Alexandria, VA: ASCD.

Wiliam, D. (2016) The Secret of Effective Feedback. *Educational Leadership*. 73 (7): 10–15.

Willis, J. (2011) Writing and the Brain: Neuroscience Shows the Pathways to Learning. Retrieved from http://www.nwp.org/cs/public/print/resource/3555.

Wilson, T. D., Reinhard, D. A., Westgate, E. C., Gilbert, D. T., Ellerbeck, N., Hahn, C. Brown, C. L., & Shaked, A. (2014). Just Think: The Challenges of the Disengaged Mind. *Science*. 345 (6192): 75–77.

Zeld, D., Cowan, R. L., Riccardi, P., Baldwin, R. M., Ansari, M. S., Li, R., Shelby, E. S., Smith, C. E., McHugo, M., & Kessler, R. M. (2008). Midbrain Dopamine Receptor Availability Is Inversely Associated with Novelty-Seeking Traits in Humans. *Journal of Neuroscience*. 28 (53): 14372–14378.

Zwiers, J., & Crawford, M. (2011). *Academic Conversations: Classroom Talk That Fosters Critical Thinking and Content Understandings*. Portland, ME: Stenhouse.

CPSIA information can be obtained
at www.ICGtesting.com
Printed in the USA
FFOW01n0654120618
47122858-49643FF

9 780415 403160